"Excuse me," he said, trying to get my attention. I ignored him and kept shopping. Damn, he was following me. A few minutes later, again, I heard, "Excuse me."

This time I couldn't ignore him. I turned around to see someone I had no interest in meeting ever in life. I looked at him, raised my eyebrows, and said, "Yes?"

"I just wanted to say hello and let you know that I think you are so beautiful," he said.

"Ok, thank you," I said and started to turn around.

"Are you married, or do you have a man?" he asked before I could walk away.

"Yes, I do," I said with a half-smile, then I turned to walk away.

That should have been the end of it, and usually, it is. But when it isn't, I start to get annoyed, and you can definitely see it on my face. Because there should be nothing else to say, I told you I am taken. And even for those who lie and say they are married and have a man when they don't, it means they are NOT interested. Right? Well, not to this guy.

"You should be my woman," he

continued. I turned around and looked at him with a Nigga, even if I wasn't married (and I'm actually not, but that's not the point), I still wouldn't want you, look. But instead of saying that, I said, "I don't think so."

Divorced & Dating

Looking for Mr. Right Finding Mr. Wrong!

GABRIELA ZION

Cover photo by j.bojorquezphotography

Published in the United States Divorced and Dating: Looking for Mr. Right Finding Mr. Wrong
Copyright © 2022 Gabriela Zion
First Edition, November 2022
ISBN: 9798373405980

This book is dedicated to my LaLa and my wise old Aunt Tillie.

Hope I made you proud.

Table of Contents

INTRODUCTION

I am not here to tell you all about the do's and don'ts of dating and relationships, and I don't claim to be some expert or relationship guru. But I am here to take you on a journey of what I've seen out here in this dating world after divorce. You can take all the advice in the world on what not to do and what to avoid, but everyone has their own mind, and we are not robots, even though I've met a few. And when dealing with matters of the heart, all that good judgment goes out the window along with some of your sanity. But that's ok because that is what makes us human, and that is what gives YOU your experiences— good ones and not-so-good ones... ok, and some really shitty, crazy ones too!

I want to take you on a ride, my ride, and may-be it will spark a conversation when you're on that first date or even date #156. Ok, maybe not that many. Hopefully, you're not on that number be- cause, damn, that's a lot of dates. Or for the fellas, when you are on that date, maybe you will think twice and not make that dumb comment that will totally change the direction of where you wanted it to go because now, she's looking at

1

you like damn, maybe you will be a little more sensitive to what she's talking about instead of looking expression- less and bored.

You will see, if you really think about it, all these little things matter in achieving your ultimate goal, whatever your goal may be. I am always looking for something special to happen, no matter who my first date is with.... that beautiful connection where you want time to stop so you don't have to part ways. I know, I want all the cliches ever invented. Sometimes I think, damn girl, aren't you a little too old to still have your head in the clouds. All I can say to that is, "No, I am not. That is what I want, and sooner or later, I am going to get it even if it kills me."

I believe you are supposed to be leading with your heart. I mean, you are out here dating. How else will you find Love if you are not open from the very beginning, right? I want to daydream of conversations we've had and remember how I felt after every kiss and every touch. I want to have moments. Moments I can relive every time I close my eyes. Ok, I know what you're thinking. Damn, that was a little too deep, and you're probably right. But I can get a lot deeper than that. Trust me.

However, I am here to tell you that just because this is what I want, and this is what is in my heart, does not ensure I will have great experiences in my search for Mr. Right. For me, it has been quite the opposite. My heart wants Movie Romance, but to tell you, in dating after divorce, I have experienced the Good, the Bad, and definitely some Ugly! Here we go on this crazy ride in my search for

Love, a Relationship, and ultimately, Marriage!

CHAPTER ONE: BACKGROUND

I am just a regular ole girl who's been dating off and on for quite some time now. I wanted to share my experiences, hoping that someone/ anyone out there could relate to them, learn from them, or at the very least, get a good laugh. I have definitely laughed out loud to keep from crying. I thought to myself, I know there have to be women or even men out there who have had interesting/ borderline crazy experiences. If not, then I think I, at the very least, deserve a pound or a high five for surviving! I believe everyone must take their own journey to get to their final destination. In my case, boy has it been a very wild and crazy journey, but nevertheless, it has been MY journey!

I'm always being asked, "Why are you still single? You must be very picky." Or, "What's wrong with you, because I know you must get asked out a lot?" My response to that is, "The same reason you or anyone else is single. I haven't found that right person who wants the same things I do, or compatibility wasn't there, chemistry or personalities didn't work together." When I'm asked such a general question, I give a broad, general answer. Just because someone is attractive doesn't mean their life is automatically perfect. We tend to deal with more issues that men throw at us. Of course, I am speaking for myself, but I have a feeling I'm not alone.

I tend to get men that seem very confident when we first meet, over messaging or over phone conversations. After that, for some reason they become insecure and think they need to be a tough guy or act like they are not that into me. For example, when I meet someone, I get, "Oh wow, your pictures don't do you justice." As time goes on, they start acting as if too many compliments or wanting to spend more time together or even buying me gifts are a bad thing. This somehow means they are kissing my ass, and they don't want to look like a Sucka. Then, they stop doing it. When in fact, this is all called DATING, SIR!

We are all looking for something if we are single. Whether it is love, a relationship, just companionship/friendship, or hook ups with no strings attached, and that's ok. There should be no judgment as long as you are upfront with your intentions, that way, there is no confusion. We all know that sometimes we don't get that honesty, and that is what screws everything up. People come in all shapes and sizes, from all different walks of life, and from all over the world. I know the older you get, this all gets more serious and very real.

When you're in your 20s, you think you have all the time in the world, and you'll never be old and alone, and you're just having fun. Then in your 30s, you're more serious about looking for a relationship but still having fun; unless you're a woman 35 and up and have no children, then you're starting to feel pressure. Then in your 40s you are straight in panic mode! You are trying to keep it together and not give off the desperate vibe, but inside you're like, "This is some Bullshit. Why am I still single?! What in the Hell is going on?" JS (Just saying).

I feel compelled to say that I in no way feel that

I am better than anyone. Everyone is entitled to their preferences, and believe it or not, my standards were a lot higher when I began my dating journey back in 2006 after my divorce. Over the years, through trial and error, lots and lots of trials, I started crossing things off of my list of things he must have, thinking that it would help my plight. Well, NO, it did not. In fact, by lowering my standards, I subjected myself to situations I could have avoided.

My thinking at the time was, "Ok maybe if lowering my requirements to a man having the basics such as a job, his own place, and a car, that should be a good start." These are things you should at least have if you are trying to date, right? Nope! I quickly found that if those were my standards, there was a certain type of guy I was going to attract, and unfortunately, not the type of man I was or am looking for. And that type of man, as crazy as it sounds, is usually missing one of those three things! I mean, I'm only asking that you have these three basic things, and you don't even have that!!! You have got to be Shittin me! WTF (what the fuck) is really going on?!

Please, keep reading, and I will have some very entertaining examples of what I'm talking about.

Ok, here we go...

RANDOM MEETINGS

I was at the gas station, minding my own business, when I heard, "Excuse me, excuse me." I think we've all heard this one. "I don't mean to bother you, but I had to stop and speak to you because you are so fine."

I just looked at him with a half-smile because I didn't want to come off like a total bitch, but I did want him to know that he was disturbing me and my minding my own business flow. I wasn't even really making eye contact because when you do, it's like a green light for him to continue. But of course, he didn't get any of that. We all know that the guys who approach a woman like that are not very attractive or not attractive at all, and they seem to be the ones with all the confidence in the world. SMH (Shaking My Head). You know what I'm talking about. Then he said, "I just had to come over and speak and see if there is any possible way I could get your number?"

So much for subtlety, right?

"Is that your car?" I asked. "Yeah."

"Do you live around here?"

"Yeah, not too far from here. I stay with my brother."

See, told you. I didn't even get to the third

9

one if he had a J.O.B. That's when I realized that if I kept thinking that was all I needed a man to have, these three basic things, that was all I was going to attract, and sometimes, not even all three. You better believe I raised my standards really fast.

Another time, I was walking through a parking lot, minding my own business, when I heard, "Excuse me, excuse me." But I kept walking because, sometimes, if I ignored them, they disappeared. But not this time. Finally, I turned around, and I saw a man walking fast to catch up to me.

"Did it hurt, did it hurt?" he said when he finally caught up.

I was looking at him with a confused look and said, "What are you talking about?"

"Did it hurt when you fell down from heaven?" he answered.

I know, I know, stupid, right. But you should have seen the look on this man's face. He was just smiling at me like it was a serious question. I couldn't help but smile.

Another time, again, I was minding my own business, as usual, walking through the same parking lot, when I heard a man speaking.

"Are you ok? Are you ok?"

Again, I had a very confused look on my face. He was looking at me, expecting an answer. I said, "Yes, I'm fine. Why wouldn't I be?"

"You look like an Angel, and I was just wondering if you were ok on the way down from heaven?" he answered, smiling.

Come on, you can't make this shit up! Lol! Suffice to say, I get pretty interesting men who approach me from time to time, and I probably should go to a different store. Lol.

Another time, I was at the grocery store, AGAIN minding my own business, when I noticed a man lurking around me.

"Excuse me," he said, trying to get my attention. I ignored him and kept shopping. Damn, he was following me. A few minutes later, again, I heard, "Excuse me."

This time I couldn't ignore him. I turned around to see someone I had no interest in meeting ever in life. I looked at him, raised my eyebrows, and said, "Yes?"

"I just wanted to say hello and let you know that I think you are so beautiful," he said.

"Ok, thank you," I said and started to turn around.

"Are you married, or do you have a man?"

he asked before I could walk away.

"Yes, I do," I said with a half-smile, then I turned to walk away.

That should have been the end of it, and usually, it is. But when it isn't, I start to get annoyed, and you can definitely see it on my face. Because there should be nothing else to say, I told you I am taken. And even for those who lie and say they are married and have a man when they don't, it means they are NOT interested. Right? Well, not to this guy.

"You should be my woman," he continued.

I turned around and looked at him with a Nigga, even if I wasn't married (and I'm actually not, but that's not the point), I still wouldn't want you, look. But instead of saying that, I said, "I don't think so." "Leave him," he said as I started to walk away.

OMG! At that point, I went into Really irritated mode. I was hoping that he did not start walking toward me because I had already started pushing my cart in the other direction. If he did, this little man and I were going to fight right here in the produce section. I saw him in the corner of my eye, kind of hesitate, but then he finally walked away. Thank goodness because I didn't want to make a scene.

But honestly, I can't be mad at a man trying to shoot his shot. Right. You never know if you don't try. But please, men out there, this is not an open invitation for every man to pull the trigger. Please keep in mind your level of attractiveness. I'm just saying, please make it make sense. Look in the mirror and make it make sense. That's all I'm saying.

Another time, I met a man, and it was totally random. One day, I stopped in a little car lot that had nice cars for sale. I was looking to upgrade my car, and I saw a black Lexus on the lot, so I decided to stop by and check it out. As I was looking at the outside of the car, a short, stalky Italian, much older than me, man came out. He had green eyes, and he looked like he was probably a handsome guy when he was younger. However, present-day he was overweight and looked like there was a small child living inside his stomach. He introduced himself to me as Peter and asked me how I liked the car. I told him I liked it and would like to see the inside. He suggested we go inside the office so he could get the keys and get a copy of my driver's license. You know, the usual protocols.

When I walked into the office, there were 3 or 4 other guys there. Peter introduced me to everyone as if it were a gathering instead of a car lot. Kind of different, but ok, I played along. I mean, shit, if it would get me a good deal on the car, what the hell. He handed me the keys and told me to take it for a spin and see how I liked it. I did just that, and I did like it. When I walked back into the office, he was smiling from ear to ear. Not sure if it was because he was about to make a sale or something else.

Once we got the paperwork started, one of the other guys offered me some water. Peter started with small talk while we waited to hear from the bank. Boy, could this Italian man talk. I wasn't even paying attention to what he was talking about, but every so often, I nodded and smiled, which is fine because we were just killing time. He asked me if I was married, and I told him no, I was divorced.

He seemed to like that answer because then he stared at me with this dumb look on his face. He asked me if I ever went to the casino. I told him I went from time to time. He told me he often went to the casino and was a "High Roller." Whatever that meant. He also wanted me to know that he was planning on going that night. I think I knew where this was going. Believe it or not, he was a funny little, round man. Pretty harmless, and he appeared to be totally smitten with me. Yes, already. Lol.

After we got all the paperwork done, I got myself a Lexus. After a couple of hours there, more like hanging out than conducting business, he mentioned again that he was going to the casino. This time, he asked me if I wanted to go with him. After thinking about it, I thought, what's the harm in going to a casino full of people with a man I just bought a car from? I mean, it wasn't like the police wouldn't know where to find him if some shit went down. He owned a car lot. So I told him, "Why not? I don't have any plans." Once we finished our business, he suggested we leave from there. I said ok because it was only 5 o'clock. I figured I'd only stay a couple of hours, and it wouldn't even be dark once I left. See, harmless.

We got to the casino and went straight to a blackjack table in the back room. The "High Roller room." Ok, I guess that meant he had the big bucks to spend. Once we sat down, they all seemed to know who Peter was. I guess he was a regular. They brought us drinks, and then Old Peter pulled out a big wad of hundreds from his pocket. I don't even know how that fit in his pocket. That's how big the wad was. He started pulling out 100s and put them on the table, so we could start playing blackjack. He gave me a couple of hundreds to start my hand too.

I was checking out the scene there. It looked like some shit out of a movie. Except for me, I kinda looked out of place. Everyone else was on the older side and not Black or Mexican, if you know what I mean. They were... uh... White. But everyone was pretty friendly to me, so I joined in. We were all drinking and laughing, and some were smoking cigars. All that money being thrown around was making my head spin. I mean, shit, if you're gonna just throw money away, you can hand it over to me. That's what I wanted to tell Old Peter, but he seemed to be having a good time. I could see this was his thing.

A couple of younger guys came over to the table. They looked at me, then at Peter. It was like some mafia shit. I guess they thought I was with him, so hands off. One of them kept looking at me, but I didn't want any problems. I'd seen Casino. I kept my eyes on the table. I won a couple of hands, but I was definitely losing more than I was winning. I was starting to feel bad because I was losing his money. Probably down $500. It was no big deal to him, but I didn't want him to get the wrong idea, so I told him I was done playing and I'd just watch.

Alright, you're probably wondering what the hell was going on here. And my answer to that is, "Nothing." I was just out having a good time at the casino. I mean, damn, everything doesn't have to be about dating. I mean, come on, I was with a round Italian man who wanted to treat me to a good time at the casino. What's the harm in that? He hadn't even tried anything, so I thought he just enjoyed my company like a lot of older men do. I didn't see anything wrong with that.

After he lost a couple of thousand dollars more, he was ready to go. We drove back to the car lot where my car was waiting for me. I told him I had a good time and thanked him for letting me hang out with him.

"No, thank you for spending your time with me. I know you must have a lot of choices," he said. Not sure what he meant, but before I could say anything, he continued, "I want to spend time with you. You are a beautiful woman, and I can treat you very well."

I had to admit, I didn't see that one coming, so I was speechless. Aside from the fact that he was old enough to be my father, I didn't even want to think about exactly what he meant by, "I want to spend time with you." I guess he saw my wheels turning, so before I could say anything, he said, "Just think about it, ok?" Then he opened my car door, reached in, and put some money in the car, and said, "Call me."

As I was stopped at the stoplight, I picked up the money and saw it was $500. Well, damn. Well, maybe I could... My inner voice said, "Stop! No Bitch, you are not a Hooker! This man is married and wants you to be his mistress." Ok... Ok... I get it. I wasn't doing that.

Well, I have to admit, I can't lie to myself. I knew damn well I could never be with him, not even for a lot of money. He was old and fat. I mean, he looked like he was 9 months pregnant. How would that even work? I never called him and never saw him again. Not even when I spent too much money shopping, and I ended up being late on my car note and could've used some extra money. You know what I mean. Nope, not even then.

CHAPTER TWO: ONLINE DATING

Dating sites, I believe, are another good way to meet people—all kinds of people... from all different backgrounds... from all different places. At least those were my initial feelings about online dating. And I, like lots of other people, don't really go out to clubs or bars very often, but when I did, I had zero luck meeting anything close to a match. Now let's see... the problem is not with dating sites, it's with people who are not truthful about who they really are on these sites.

Ok, I get that you are pretty much trying to sell yourself, so you are going to build yourself up. Unfortunately, you are not going to know what a person is really like just from reading what they wrote or if everything they've said about themselves is even true unless you spend time around that person and get to know them. But I believe that applies to anyone regardless of where you meet, not just people you meet online. The problem for me has been embellishing what you have, who you really are, and most importantly, WHAT YOU ACTUALLY LOOK LIKE RIGHT NOW!!!

Ok, don't act like LOOKS aren't the most important thing when dating online. I am not saying their pictures are fake, like getting catfished, because that shit is real and no joke. I've seen the show! But don't act like looks don't matter because we all know that they absolutely do. The people who say they don't matter are probably not that attractive. Trust me, the good-looking people absolutely think they matter.

Sometimes pictures are a little bit deceiving. For example, picture taking is an art. If you know what you're doing, pictures can be amazing. There are many factors that contribute to a great picture, such as the right camera phone, angles, and lighting. Oh, and people using that damn filter bullshit. I have no idea how that even works, so I am not guilty of that. But I hear this is a big complaint for men. I hear you, fellas. I totally agree that's some bullshit too. I get it.

There is also a range of attractiveness… Sorry people, these are real subjects in the dating world that no one wants to talk about. There are also levels of attractiveness. Yes, there are. There is Beautiful, Very Attractive, Attractive, Average, Not Ugly, and Ugly. In a perfect world, no one would judge you by your looks, but we all know that's exactly what happens. The more attractive you are, the more options you have as far as who you want to date and pretty much in life. And also, the more your inbox gets filled up. Just saying.

Ok, first, let us address the elephant in the room...PICTURES. My stance on pictures is this: you fall into only three (3) categories always, NO exceptions:

You look just/exactly like your picture(s).

You look better than your picture(s).

You look worse than your picture(s). That's it... think about it... you know I'm right.

Ok, for me, I don't care what anyone says, in the beginning, looks matter. Call me shallow or whatever you want. There MUST be an initial attraction for me to even be interested in getting to know that you're an amazing guy. I guess people feel differently about this and believe that inner beauty is the most important thing. Well, I'm not saying that what's on the inside is not important at some point. I'm saying, I have

22

to like what you look like on the outside first in order for me to even care what you are like on the inside. I'm all for brutal honesty. And believe it or not, I have a variety of tastes. I'm not just attracted to one type of guy. Ok, the other thing is, when a guy says, "Give me a chance, come on, don't be shallow," or "looks shouldn't be that important, right?" Hmmm, ok, well, let's see. You're telling me not to be shallow. But... umm... excuse me, Sir, aren't you trying to talk to me because of my looks? Right!

Why do I say that, or how do I know that, you ask? Well, let's see, the messages I received read:

Mark ⋮

Hello how are u? Most beautiful woman on POF no doubt respect!!

7:50 PM

9:41 PM

 ImHim39 ⋮

Gabbriala... all due respect but u like sumthin special... u got da glow n so sexy with it.. have a dopeassday beautiful

12:07 PM

 3PHOENIXSON9 ⋮

You're so Beautiful Hello

3:16 PM

24

Damon :

I DESIRE a sincerely seeking woman who's still fun loving...

If that's U then let's make it happen XxXpeditiously.!.

TIME awaits for NO one My Loveliness. It's definitely OUR most VALUABLE ASSet. WE really don't know how much of it we have left.!.!. ONLY the Big Guy in the sky knows that so yes I'm an XxXpediteR I don't BELIEVE in wasting precious time (mine or yours)...

I'm currently available at the moment but I'm looking, dating and entertaining and I CERTAINLY enjoy your look therefore I'm perhaps interested in an opportunity at your love so let's C. Is this asking for too much or is this ok with U?

5:58 AM

That's why. How is that fair to me? Look, I just want to feel the same toward you as you feel toward me and have the same attraction, or it's just not going to work for me long term. Ok, say I give you a chance, and you are indeed a wonderful person, but if I'm not attracted to you, your Wonderfulness is not going to make me want to Fuck you just because you are a wonderful person. I'm sorry, but my Pussy is still gonna be saying, "NOPE. KEEP THAT UGLY DICK AWAY FROM ME!" I know... I know... I know... there's that brutal honesty again. Sorry about that.

Example

I responded to a message. He asked for my number, so we exchanged numbers. We set up a lunch date for the next day. Ok, you're probably wondering what it was about this guy that made me want to respond? Well, his pictures were ok. He was retired from the military, was a local guy, had no kids, and he was my age, so he wasn't trying to have kids at this age. I thought he seemed like a nice guy who had his shit together. I know what you're thinking, what about the looks part you were saying was so important? Well, I didn't say that I never

26

tried putting that aside and give it a try, so this was one of those times when I looked at everything, not just the looks.

In the short messages we exchanged, he seemed like a really nice guy, and he was really selling himself with places he had traveled, his career, what he was looking for, which was a wife to love and share everything with and take care of. Blah, Blah, Blah. You know, everything most women want to hear. I guess I was a little naïve back then. I was thinking, ok, he has the security, he has no kids, and he is my age, and he is retired from the military (ok, that means benefits!). As long as he's decent looking, I'm good. So I thought.

During our conversations, we were trying to come up with a spot that was mutually convenient because we decided on a lunch date, and I had to go back to work afterward. I could only do an hour to an hour and a half. He suggested Applebee's. Yup, Applebee's. That told me a couple of things: he was really not trying to impress me on the first meeting, and he was a simple guy (sad face because I'm so not a simple kinda girl), or he really had no clue. Well, I just agreed and said, "Ok, that's fine." When I got there, I got a text saying he was running a little late (another sad face). All kinds of things started running through my mind. Mainly, that this was a lunch date during the week, and I had to go back to work, so I needed to move it along. Second, let me look at his pictures again (probably shouldn't have done that because he was not looking that great anymore... damn, or maybe he never did).

He texted me as he pulled up, so I kept my eye on the door. At this point, I was still trying to be hopeful even though he was very late, and I was probably going to have to take my shit to go. A couple of guys came through the door, who were not him cuz my guy was Black not White or Mexican. Ok, the door opened again, and it's a Black guy. Damn, and he's looking like the pics I just saw. SHIT... He was a #3 remember, "you look worse than your pictures. Ok, here we go.

Hey, how's it going, blah, blah, blah. We exchanged pleasantries, and he seemed very pleased because he said, "Wow, you look better than your pictures," (a #2). He had this dumb look on his face, a cross between shock and Damn, I just hit the Lotto! The look on my face was, "No, Nigga, you didn't!" My natural reaction was to keep talking, so it didn't become awkward, and I didn't want him to feel bad because I didn't feel the same about him (because it's not his fault I wasn't interested).

He kept apologizing for being late, then started really selling himself. How ready he was for a wife, about his career, but all I heard at this point was Wah, Wah, Wah. He told me that I looked much better in person and how happy he was that I responded to him on the site. I thanked him and tried to redirect the conversation to generalizations such as where you're from, where have you traveled, things of that nature, so he didn't try to get too personal. I do have this ability to make men feel at ease in such a way that they feel very comfortable, and how I know is because, by the end of any date, they think that I'm actually into them too and think I want to see them again. But unfortunately, it's normally A NO FOR ME, DOG! (Damn, that Randy Jackson!)

Alright, it was time to wrap this up, and this is the part I hate. Parting ways without having to lie because I hate lying — even little white lies. He walked me to my car, and so it didn't get any more awkward for ME than it already was. I quickly thanked him for lunch, and I gave him a short, reachy hug. You know the kind.

"So, can I see you again? he asked. "Just

text me," I said quickly.

I got in my car in a hurra and left. The only way I can look at situations like this is, well, at least he fed me.

I got a text shortly after (which I expected), saying what a great time he had and that I was just the kind of girl he'd always wanted. Great, now I felt bad because he couldn't help the way he looked, and he looked just like a lost puppy dog. Awww, he was such a nice guy. Well, maybe we could be friends. No! No! No! Stop it! I was looking for a relationship, not a friendship. Damnit! Ok, I've got to get thicker skin because I don't want to be guilted into dating someone. SMH (shaking my head). That wasn't that bad, right?

My advice here is that there is nothing wrong with going out with someone and becoming their friend, but don't lead them on into thinking more is coming when you feel nothing. I had to finally send him the text. You know the one… "It was nice meeting you, and you seem like a really good/nice guy, however, I just don't think we are a match. Good luck to you."

I hate having to do that, but it is necessary when they keep calling and texting even though you don't respond. I mean, shit, why, why, why do I have to say anything? No response is a response! Thank the Lord, after about 5 unanswered text messages, he finally got it. I had a couple more of those dates then it really got interesting.

Example

I was online dating and trying to find someone local (Arizona) because you will soon see that most of my relationships/dating have been with out of state men. I ran across Jason. He was alright, an attorney and local. I sent him a message. I have never been the type to wait until I get a message. If I have an interest, I send a message. My opening message was always, "Hey there, how's it going?" Yup, that's it, every time. Lol. They either respond, or they don't, and believe me, there have been some that did not respond. See, it happens to all of us. Nothing is ever a sure thing. Anyway, Jason responded, and we chit-chatted a bit. Until I said, of course, "Here's my number if you wanna talk." Remember, dragging this chatting longer than needed is annoying to me.

He called, and we chit-chatted a bit. The conversation was ok. Nothing earthshattering, but enough for me to want to meet up for drinks.

Ok, full disclosure... the state I was in was that I was kind of getting burned out not being able to find anyone I was interested in and/or attracted to. I'm not saying that I lowered my standards, however, maybe I had in the looks department. Just being completely honest. I was starting to look at other areas that might work, you know careers, stability, location, things of that nature. Right or wrong, that's where my head was at.

Ok, back to Jason. He was a lawyer, so I know what you're thinking... pretty perfect, right? He's a lawyer, and I'm a paralegal... perfect. We'll see.

I first made a couple of suggestions of a meeting spot to no avail because he suggested we meet at a sports bar between my place and his. I said, "Ok, that's cool." What was really going through my mind was, ok, this is our first meeting, and you don't want to drive too far out of your way? That told me that he was not very accommodating to a woman. He didn't really care about making a good first impression, and that told me that he was probably all about making his life easier. Typical lawyer shit.

Trust me, I've been around them long

enough to know. They have a lot of similar ways about them. I got to the bar, and he was already there. I saw him sitting in a booth, and he was on the short side, but since I am only 5'5", not a big deal. I mean, everyone should be taller than me, right. Unless you're a midget, excuse me, little person. Lol. We had a drink, and I don't remember if we ordered appetizers or not. But probably not, because it was a short meeting. We talked a little about our backgrounds and if we had kids. We both did, but his one kid was only a baby!!!! No, not the 40 and a baby. Shit... Abort the mission... I Repeat, ABORT THE MISSION!!! My youngest was definitely not a baby, and I was totally done with little babies and anything similar to anything, well, you know, baby. Aside from the fact that I felt absolutely nothing, and the only thing I found attractive about this man was that he was a lawyer and lived in Arizona, this was definitely not a recipe for success. I should also point out that I didn't think he was all that interested in me either. I mean, aside from when I came in, he did say, "Oh, wow, you look just like your pictures." That was pretty much it. If he was interested, I couldn't tell. Maybe he felt that I wasn't feeling him at all. I don't know, but whatever the case, it was not a match. We finished our drinks, and he said we should get together again, and I said, "sounds good." But I think we both knew we would never see each other again.

See, not everybody likes me either. Lol. But what I learned here is that no matter if you are frustrated, tired, or burned out from dating, if you lower your standards, it will affect finding that perfect match you are looking for. You are going to end up with someone that only has a few things you like about them, and that's never going to be enough.

Example

How about this one? This was a date from the dating site Black People Meet (BPM). Gotta luv that Black People Meet. Lol. I was browsing, and here was one, Jeff. The opening line was not too crazy, his pictures looked pretty good. So I responded, and then he responded, "Thank you for responding to my messages." A little bit of an eager beaver, but here we go. He was a local, so that was good. He asked for my number. I like a man who takes the initiative and is forward, not aggressive (there is a difference). We started chit-chatting, and then we set a time to meet up.

I got to the restaurant, and he was already there. What I saw when I walked in was a tall, light-skinned man wearing a turtleneck sweater, Timberlands and a bubble/puffer jacket vest. I guess they are called bubble jackets. I think. The reason I am describing what he was wearing, is because we were in Arizona, and yes, it was winter, but we were not in New York or Chicago where it snows. His attire was kind of overkill. Just saying. He was tall, about 6'2"-6'3", a little overweight. I was sure he was well over 200 lbs. because he seemed huge next to little ole me. Again, remember I'm 5'5", and at that time, I weighed about 135-138 lbs. See, kinda huge. The reason I bring up he was a little overweight is because during our conversations, he talked about how he worked out regularly and hiked and was very active, running marathons and shit. When I saw him, I expected to see him looking like he was in shape or at least looking like his pictures which would match that description. Well, not from what I was seeing in front of me. He was a #3. The pictures he had posted were definitely not current. SMH (shaking my head).

Jeff saw me and was more than delighted.

35

He kept complimenting me, and my first response was to smile and thank him. But after 50 of them, I was like, ok, ok, stop, please.

Normally, I go with the flow, and even if I am not interested, which I was not, I still am very polite and finish the date. I hate when I hear people say, "Why did you stay? You should have just left, especially if he didn't look like his picture(s)." I mean, unless it's a totally different person, then I would definitely leave. However, I would never leave because it wasn't a match. He can't help what he looks like. I feel like there is nothing wrong with having drinks or dinner with someone and just enjoying good company. Although I will never lead anyone on, I also will never be rude and make him feel bad or make him think he is not good enough. I mean, shit, it's just not a match. And if you can't afford to pay for dinner, then you should have never invited me to dinner. Nigga, you know your pockets better than I do.

Ok, back to the date. Our conversations were Pretty good, and we had things in common. We were laughing, but again the key for me was to not make him so comfortable that he thought that this was going somewhere. From what I could see, he was not going to get my subtle hints. We ordered food, and it was ok. I mean, it wasn't a five-star restaurant or anything, and if he thought it was, then that was another problem about him. We both liked sports and loved basketball. I told him about the time I took my son to a Suns game during All-Star Weekend here in Arizona, whatever year that was.

The Suns were playing the Bulls, so I took my young son to the game because he was into Derrick Rose at the time. I got pretty good seats next to the tunnel, just so he could get a high five from Derrick Rose. Well, it didn't quite turn out that way. It was half-time, and the Bulls were losing (dammit). The Bulls players started walking toward the tunnel. I grabbed my son and pulled his hand out because he was a little guy at the time, like 5 or 6, so when the Bulls players passed by, they could give him a high five.

Ok, here they come. Really, all they could see was me holding out a little hand, but that's ok, that should have been enough... Right. Nope. Derrick Rose came toward us, and he looked right at me. Then he looked at my son's little hand that I had pulled out of his little socket trying to get it to reach him, and he just walked right on by. Muthafucker!

Joakim Noah was behind him and saw what I was doing, and he looked at me and smiled and gave him five, and so did a couple more players after him. That was pretty cool. The people in my row were smiling and happy that we got some fives, but they also said that it was pretty shitty of Derrick Rose. So much for being a role model.

After the game, I was hoping they would beat the Suns, so maybe Derrick Rose would be in a better mood. But nope, they didn't. They flipping lost to the Suns. I said, "Ok, son, we are going to do it again, and maybe this time he gives you five." But NOPE. Same shit. He looked at me and passed us right on by. And this time, Noah paused longer than the first time and again gave him a high five and looked at me and smiled, but I was like, "No, nigga, keep walking. I'm with my son." Lol.

After I finished my story, Jeff said, "Well, I'm not mad at him, he was probably tired, and he just lost." WTF!!! You're kidding me, right? But nope, he was not. He continued with, "I really don't see anything wrong with what he did. These basketball players are not role models if they don't want to be." SMH...

"Excuse me? I don't give a shit if he feels

like he is or not. I paid a lot for those tickets just to see him, you crazy muthafucker." I didn't say that, but I did say, "Come on, if you don't care that he may have crushed a little kid's dreams, then there is something wrong with you," and I left it at that. At this point, I was no longer engaged in any conversations. I was distant, with long pauses and a lot of awkward silence on my part. But, oh well, you dummy, who doesn't know that that was not the way to get me to keep talking to you. Even if you didn't agree with me (even though every person I repeated this story to said that was very shitty of him to do that to a little kid), it was probably not a good idea to voice that. You know, being that you were trying to get with me. Now, I don't even want to be your "friend" because you have just shown me you have no compassion. So, fuck you!

Not too much longer, it was time for me to go. In this case, there should have been no question that I was NOT interested. At least so I thought. Because as soon as I left and started driving home, I got a text saying how much he enjoyed our date. SMH. I also got a text the next morning, the next night, and a few voicemails about how it was great meeting me and what a wonderful time he had. Boy, I tell you, sometimes I just have no words.

After a couple of weeks of texts and invitations to random places, he finally got the hint and stopped calling. Ok, so in this case, I don't know what my lesson was, except just cut it off fast and swift.

Example

Here is another date. Again, met him online, started messaging then chit-chatting. He was a local guy. We set up a date because you know how I feel about wasting time. We decided to meet up downtown at a bar. I don't like meeting downtown unless I'm already with someone because of the parking situation. It's a nightmare for me trying to find parking on the street, which you rarely do, or then have to park in a garage. I probably should have read parking for dummies because sometimes I don't even know how I manage to lose my car. But I do. Anyway, this is no different.

I couldn't find the place, so Gary talked me through to where the bar was. In my defense, the bar was tucked away and upstairs, so it wasn't like you could see it off the street. I was then forced to park in a garage around the corner from the bar. Once

I started walking, I found someone to ask. I finally found it.

It was not the dead of winter, but it was not spring either. When I walked up to who I believed was Gary, I saw he was wearing shorts and a short- sleeve polo shirt. I was dressed in jeans, a top with a long sleeve sweater because the temperature was in the low 60s. When I saw him in those wrinkled shorts, I thought, shit, okaaaay, here we go.

First of all, when I saw him, he was definitely overweight. I am not exaggerating because our first conversation was him telling me about how he'd gained a bunch of weight, and he was trying to get back down to his normal size. If I was a total bitch, I would have pointed out the obvious. Why don't you have current pictures up, fat boy? And did you airbrush your shit because your pictures did not reflect any craters on your face! Ok, Ok, Ok, sorry... but shit, come on. Was that not deceit??? I thought. I even put on my profile these are my current pictures, so have current pictures on yours.

Why don't people follow the rules? Damn.

Remember when I said I don't walk out on dates? Well, I didn't start now either. He seemed like a nice guy. Let me just say, I sometimes have this problem of feeling bad even though I shouldn't, especially when they tell me their story. I start to look at them and say, well, maybe they're not that bad. I mean, if he lost his weight and smoothed his face out, he would be fine. Right?

Why? Why? Why, Lord Jesus, do you do this to me? Ok, snap out of it, pull yourself together. Whenever I do this, and by this, I mean try to make excuses as to why I should overlook what's really in front of me, my inner voice always seems to bring me back to reality. "Bitch, please look at him, it's too much work for even him to do. Don't you think if he was really wanting to make these changes, he would have done it already?" Ok, Ok, ok, I get it. I snapped out of that thinking and got back to the reality of the date.

We talked about where we were from. I know, blah, blah, blah. I was really tired of repeating myself and telling my story when I went on these damn dates. It was exhausting, but that's the name of the game, right.

I remember telling him about myself on the phone, but when it came to him talking about his career/job he said he would explain it to me when we met. I know, that's not kinda creepy at all. Now I know why he didn't want to say anything on the phone. He told me he had a company that he came up with selling Vitamins to enhance your libido — kinda like Viagra, but in the form of "Vitamins." Right, that's what I said. Lol. He started explaining how it all started. He was having problems himself with his hormones, and he was a young guy, so he did some experimenting... and voila, he came up with these vitamins. I think he may have even showed me a packet of them. He then talked about how well he was doing and that he did most of his business overseas, mainly in the Middle East— Dubai, to be exact. How he traveled there a lot and would like to have someone to travel with. I know what you're thinking... you're not falling for this shit, are you? Well, I mean, he sounded very believable. And why couldn't he have all the things he said he had? There was my inner voice again. "Bitch, why are his clothes wrinkled right now?!?! Because he has so much money, he just didn't feel like having them dry cleaned or ironed!" Ok, ok, you might have a point there. Whatever, let us just move on. I ordered food, we had drinks, and we had some good conversation. But that was going to be it for Big Ole Gary.

The only question right now was, was I going

to remain friends with him? We'll see. Because he was saying he was ok with that. And, of course, that made me feel even worse. I knew he knew that his appearance was not getting him anywhere. I finished my drink, and it was time to go. He offered to walk me to my car.

"I'm parked in a garage around the corner."

"Ok, well, I drove here with my cousin. He's over there waiting," he told me.

"Wait a minute. You mean he's been here waiting for you this whole time?"

"Yeah, we're supposed to be going somewhere after, so he rode with me."

I thought to myself, that's a little weird, especially since you're a dude not a female needing a chaperone. And he's been sitting here for a couple of hours. Now, it is definitely a no to being friends. Weirdo. But whatever, I just needed to get to my car.

For some reason, I felt he was a harmless, overweight guy that was insecure about himself. Those were the vibes I got, so I was not worried at all. When his friend pulled up in an old van, I knew he didn't have shit! This was some bullshit right here. Dubai, my ass. SMDH. His cousin told me they had a carpet cleaning business and that's where the van came into play. At that point, just get me to my car. His "cousin" was very polite, and we drove to my car without incident. Lol. He told me he hoped he could see me again, and I gave him a hug goodbye, got in my car, and drove away. See, told you, harmless.

You're probably wondering what's going through my mind right about now. Well, I was getting worn down with all the misinformation, deceiving conversations, and lies. I was looking at myself and wondering what it was about me that I kept attracting crazy ass men. I mean, how was I asking for all this bullshit? I guess I could be thankful I was attracting stupid, crazy, not deranged, psycho, crazy. But that didn't make me feel better. I needed to take a little break for a minute and regroup. And that's what I did.

CHAPTER THREE:

INTERMISSION

While on my little hiatus, I had an interesting encounter. Not even an encounter, just more interactions with men. Totally unexpected encounters. Well, a lot of them were totally unexpected. I think I mentioned how, at times, I was oblivious when a man liked me. Well, here's one of those times.

I was still married at the time and working for an attorney, Kevin, in the East Valley. The attorney I worked for was trying to get me to sign up for some type of life insurance. He not only wanted to sell me life insurance, but he also wanted me to think about getting into selling it as well. My first response was, hold on there patna, I am not a salesperson and would be horrible at it. He ignored me and still wanted to set up a meeting with the guy he knew that turned him on to selling. I believe he was a Mormon because so was

Kevin. Not that that's a big deal, he just told me that was where he knew him from, his church. Just stating facts. His name was Jason, and it was his company Kevin told me. I told him again I would not be a good salesperson at all. I was not social. I barely like talking to our clients at the office.

"It's easy, just wait until the meeting so we can explain everything to you," he said.

I said, ok (I thought to myself do I really have a choice? I mean, he is my boss) what the hell.

One evening, Kevin and Jason came to my home in Gilbert, Arizona. Kevin was a short and nerdy type with glasses, about 5 or 6 years older than me. I had only been working for him for about 4 months. Every time I went into his office, he put his arms above his head. I guess so I could see his arm muscles. I laughed in my head because it was kinda sad if he really thought that was doing anything for him. Anyway, Jason was about Kevin's age, about 6 feet, I don't know what his weight was, but he was in pretty good shape from what I could see through his business casual attire. He was a good-looking, white guy. He began to tell my husband and me about his business of selling life insurance. It sounded good but I still didn't think I was a salesperson. After about an hour, they wrapped it up and thanked us for our time.

The next day at work, Kevin asked me, "So, what did you think?" I told him I thought it was a good opportunity to get involved in life insurance. After him pressuring me into going to a meeting with Jason, I gave in. I guess I thought about it, and at that time, I was looking to make extra money.

I got to the meeting, and I saw Jason talking and mingling with other people. There were about 10 people there, including myself. He saw me, came over to me and shook my hand, and said, "I'm glad you decided to come." I smiled and said, "I just wanted to come and check out everything you were talking about, and maybe it's something I can get into." He said, "Absolutely, you can." Kevin told me, "You are a very bright woman, and he thinks you would do amazing. So, please, have a seat anywhere, and we'll get started."

I had to admit, it was pretty interesting. Something about a Series 7 license and life insurance. Interesting, but it still all sounded like Chinese to me. I guess it was one of those things where you sign up, then you try to get other people involved, but you need that Series 7 license to really make money.

Over the next month, I went to meetings, and I dragged my sister to one as well. During this particular meeting, I brought her, and at that time, I provided the name and a number of another prospect to Jason. A realtor I met who was selling us our house — a young guy who was doing well in the real estate world. At this meeting, there was me, my sister, a couple of other guys, and Jason. Jason was making the call to show us how to try and get the prospect to come to a meeting. You know, sales shit. Jason made the call. I don't remember his name so let's call him Matt. Matt answered, and Jason introduced himself and told him that he got his number from me, Gabriela. "She tells me you know her through a real estate dealing," he said.

"Oh, yeah, Gabriela and her husband, Cory. Right. Gabriela..." with a pause. "Oh, yeah, she is pretty hot, and if she wasn't married, I would definitely ask her out."

Oh, yeah, FYI, he had him on speaker so everyone in the room could hear the conversation. My sister put her hand over her mouth, trying to hold her laughter in. Jason was looking at me, and all I could do was raise my eyebrows and kind of smile. But it really didn't matter because it was pretty fuckin awkward. I had no idea he felt that way about me. He never flirted with me or even looked interested in me. After he finished the call, my sister looked at me and laughed. What I was thinking at that moment was, damn, did he just say that out loud? SMH.

Anyway, during that period, my husband and I

were at the ending stage of our marriage and just about at the point of no return. I went to work, and a few times, Kevin tried to counsel me about it, which I appreciated, but it was no use. Maybe that's why I was trying to get involved in something else to try to take my mind off my personal problems. I think it helped for a little while.

I continued to go to meetings 2 or 3 times a week. It was pretty cool meeting new people from all different walks of life. One night after a meeting, Jason and I started talking about our lives, and I mentioned that I played tennis. He said, "Oh wow, I play too. My gym has tennis courts if you want to play." I said, "I haven't played in a while, but I would luv to get back to playing again." So, we left the meeting and decided to meet up at his gym in a couple of hours, which was in the middle of where we both lived, so that was good.

We got to the gym around the same time. I was wearing what they now call yoga pants—I still call them stretch pants—and a t-shirt. I was in pretty good shape. Fit but not because I work out on the regular or eat healthily. It's pretty much by accident. (I am 5'5, 138 lbs., and shapely...so, I have a little something something, but I'm definitely not a big booty Judy type). I know you hate me, don't you? Lol.

When we got inside the gym, we found out that that location did not have tennis courts. Damn, just my luck, we picked the one location that didn't have courts. Some Bull! He suggested since we were already there, we play a game of racquetball. I said, "Ok, but I totally suck at racquetball. Definitely not the same thing as tennis." The one time I tried racquetball was with my brother, and I almost killed myself. No lie. I guess here I go again. We played a short game, and I mean short because I almost collapsed a few times, and to avoid any further embarrassment, I cried, "Uncle." As we were walking out of the racquetball court, he said, "You want to go to the pool?" I said, "Is it even still open? It's like 9 o'clock?" We went outside to check, didn't see anyone around, so we ended up sitting outside and talking.

I know you're probably wondering, what the hell was going on here? And the answer is nothing. We were just two people getting to know each other. He was married, and I was going through a divorce, but that was it. A couple of weeks went by, and I got my own place. See, getting divorced.

One day, I got a call from Jason saying he had heard about my pending divorce, and he wanted to check on me to make sure I was ok. I thought that was nice of him. Until one day he called and said he was in the neighborhood and asked if he could stop by. I happened to not be at work that day, so I said, "yeah" I figured he just wanted to talk and make sure I was doing ok.

He came over, but I noticed he was acting a little different this time. Like a little more suggestive, especially the way he was looking at me. I kept ignoring it and I acted like I didn't hear when he said, "I really want to kiss you right now." But he then looked right at me and said again, "I really want to kiss you." This time it was more of a statement like I'm going to kiss you. Maybe a part of me wanted him to. But I would have never acted on anything, well, you know, because we were both married.

So, he did. He kissed me. It was nothing like what I expected it would be. I thought maybe it would be kind of dramatic, you know, like in the movies. He pulled me close to him and caressed my face, looking into my eyes before he brushed his lips over mine. The heat of our bodies quickly ignited the fire, and next thing you know... Ok hold it, that's not what happened, so put it back in your pants. It was very awkward and kind of like this pecking then it was fast and then... and then I had to stop it because we were both married! I pulled away, and he tried coming closer to me, but I kept moving backward. I said, "You should probably go." He looked at me and said, "Really?" I was thinking, what in the ADULTERATED HELL is going on here? "Yes, Jason, you really should," I said. He then said, "You know what, you're probably right. I am really sorry."

He left, and I was totally in shock. More shocked that he was such a horrible kisser but happy he was because who knows what might have happened if he wasn't. I mean, ok, maybe he flirted with me a little, but I never thought that was going to happen at all. But it did, and that was the end of my sales career because I never went back to any meetings. I told Kevin that it just wasn't for me. I know, crazy, right? At least, I thought so.

CHAPTER FOUR: CHICAGO

Now that I had some online dating experience under my belt, I felt like it was time to get back out there and find my man. Positivity is everything, right? Here are a few stories of relationships that came out of online dating.

CHICAGO

I have never been opposed to dating a man in another state. My thinking about this is, why not? I like to travel, and I'll get to see different states and places I've never been to. That being said, I dated a guy from Chicago.

I met Dion on the dating site BPM. He was a Chicago native. I had never been to Chicago but always wanted to visit the Windy City.

I was sifting through messages and pictures, and I ran across Dion. His picture was only half of his face, so that caught my attention. Why only half a picture? Are you hiding? And if you're hiding from someone, then why are you on here? Half a picture kind of makes you stand out even more. Nevertheless, I was interested. We started exchanging messages and then numbers. Again, messaging gets old for me really quickly. We finally connected on the phone, and, of course, I asked him, "What's up with your picture or lack thereof." He said he worked for a Fortune 500 company and didn't want any problems with his company (whatever that meant). It kind of made sense because when I dated Dion, it was back in 2006ish when dating on the internet was still fairly new, so ok. Anyway, we had conversations, and over a couple of weeks, we decided we wanted to meet. I said I would go there because I told him I'd always wanted to see Chicago, and he loved that idea. I made plans to fly out for a weekend. (FYI: Every guy I dated out of state NEVER paid or even offered to buy my ticket... not ONE!)

I landed in Chicago, and Dion picked me up from the airport in his older Nissan Altima. I know you're asking why did I point out what kind of car he had? Well, come on, let's be real. I'm sure I'm not the only one who thinks to themselves, I hope he has a nice car... right? Well, if I am, screw you! He picked me up curbside, and with a quick hug hello, we were on our way.

He started with, "WOW! You look better in person." I thanked him for the compliment. (Ok, disclosure; for some reason, in the beginning, when I meet someone, they seem to be attractive to me, but after some time of dating or after it doesn't work out, they just don't look the same. I think back, and I say, "OMG, is this the same person I was dating?!?!?" And that's not a good OMG. I guess the good looks that I wanted to see wear off, and the reality is that maybe they simply weren't there to begin with... JS).

Anyway, we were driving, and I was taking in the sites on our way to his apartment in a suburb of Chicago. We got to his apartment, and it was a very nice modern new building of about 200 or so in a nice area. I was always checking out my surroundings. I was not trying to get caught up in any crazy situations, especially because of the high crime associated with Chicago that I'd always heard about. We arrived, and I put my suitcase away and got settled in, and we decided to have a quick dinner because he had planned for us to go out dancing later that night. Sounded good to me. I luv a man with a plan.

We walked across the street, where there were various restaurants to choose from. We decided on one and headed that way. At this point, I was taking in my surroundings, enjoying being out, and it felt good. It was late July or early August, so the weather was pretty good, a bit humid, but very nice. As we enjoyed our dinner, we started with general conversation and got to know each other better. I was having a good time, and it was going very well. There was some flirting going on, some laughing, and a little hugging too. Now we headed back to his place to get ready to hit the streets. (For those who don't know, that means get ready to go out to a club or nightlife! Lol.)

We changed and got ready. He said it was a casual spot, so it didn't take very long to be ready. We headed to the garage, and he said, "We'll take my other car," which was a new Corvette. Well, Ok... nice! He said he didn't drive it all the time. In my head, I was thinking, why wouldn't you pick me up in this instead of your raggedy car? I don't get it. But whatever.

We got to the spot, which looked like a good crowd of people, so that was good. It was a mixed crowd, excuse me, I mean a diverse crowd. Lol. Once we were inside, it was more on the white side, but ok, given the area we were in. As long as we could get some good music, then I didn't care. But I'm not gonna lie, I luv Black, Black, Black. Me being Mexican and Black, I luv the R&B/Hip Hop vibe.

Dion got us drinks, and I started sipping and sipping. It was not long before I was feeling good. We danced, and maybe I was feeling really good because I was not noticing his lack of dancing and instead a lot of bouncing and jumping up and down. I guess because it was now crowded, and everyone else seemed to be doing the same. Next thing I knew, someone bumped into him and spilled a little of his drink, and his reaction was RAGE! The girl was pretty apologetic, but he was extremely annoyed and started to go off on the girl. I tried to get in the middle and tried to pull him away so we could walk away, but it was not working. It took a lot more effort to get him to finally let it go. Not sure what he thought he was going to accomplish by attacking a woman for accidentally spilling his drink in a crowded club, but at least he was finally over it.

We were back to our good vibes again, and we were dancing close, hugging, and kissing a little. Things were going well. It was getting really late, and I was wiped out, so we decided to head out. He paid the valet, and we headed back to his place.

Sooo, we were still on kind of a high from the alcohol, each other, and the moment. I know you're asking, "Well, what happened? Did you do it or not?" And, well, my answer is, "A lady never tells." Hahaha JK... I am very grown...I am not embarrassed. I'm a-live-in-the-moment kinda girl. If it feels right at the time, I have no regrets... Ain't no shame in my game.

A couple of weeks went by, and he told me he had to go to California for work, and he suggested that I meet him there. So that was exactly what I did. In a couple of weeks, I caught a flight to California. Oh I take back what I said, Dion bought my ticket to Cali. for this meeting. Dion picked me up from the airport in his rental, and we headed to the hotel. We were staying at the Mission Inn in Riverside. That is right up my alley since I am from San Bernardino/Riverside. I had never stayed there, but I had been to the restaurant inside the hotel, and it is really nice. I was excited to see the inside of the hotel. And I must say, it was amazing. Beautifully landscaped, the shrubbery, flowers, everything was beautiful. I did a little research on it and found out that the Reagans had stayed here, Will and Jada, and a bunch of other old-timers.

We got to the room, and it had kind of old-world charm. Very nice. We had a romantic dinner, and after dinner, we took a walk on the grounds. I mean, it was some shit out of one of my romance novels. I was luving it. I was very turned on, so we took the party back to our room. We were so in the moment, really feeling each other... and again, I am grown, so it was time for grown-up activities. So, bye (Door closes here).

After a wonderful night, we said goodbye, and I headed back to Arizona. As soon I got up in the air, I realized I'd left my phone at the hotel!!! Damn. You know that feeling, like someone just punched you in the gut. Right. This is the age where no one carries a phone book anymore. Your cell phone is your phone book. SMH. Well, nothing I could do now because I didn't even know his phone number. I got to work the next day, and guess who left me a message? Yup, Dion. Good thing I didn't have a password lock on my phone, and he looked up my work number. We had a laugh, and he told me he was going to overnight my phone to me along with my draws I left there too. For those of you who don't know what that means, UNDERWEAR; draws is underwear. Lol.

Apparently, I left those too.

I got back to reality, and we were in constant communication, so I was planning to get out to Chicago again the following month. I was hoping my second visit would be as good as the first. I loved the anticipation. Just when you think you're gonna die from waiting for the day to come, it's here. So, off I go to Chicago. Very happy to see Dion and Chicago.

The next day he had tickets for us to go to a Cubs game. Normally, baseball is not my sport, but with good company, I'm game. Unfortunately, it wasn't the greatest time. The seats were really close together, and they were right next to the pole, so not a good view. Alright, and little did I know this was going to be a very eventful day. Keep reading, you'll see what I mean.

Dion suggested we hang out in Wrigleyville following the game, which is the surrounding areas filled with bars. I was ok with that since we were already there, and I was ok with a low-key night. After the game, we were walking down the streets and found a bar or ten! During that time, we were still having good conversations and chit-chatting, so we went into a bar where there was karaoke. At this point, we are having a pretty good time, and no, I did not participate in karaoke. We had a couple of drinks and decided to hit another bar.

By the time we left the first bar, the streets were full of people like there was a parade going on. I mean, there were people everywhere. I was so taken back by how crowded it was everywhere I looked. I asked him, "What is happening out here?" He said, "Nothing, this is Wrigleyville!" I was very overwhelmed, to say the least. I guess if you're from Chicago and go to baseball games, you know what I'm talking about. It's loud, people are drinking and drunk, and it's just madness. Like Mardi Gras. Ok, here is where the eventful part I was talking about happens.

He said he had to use the bathroom, so we went into the nearest bar and headed to the bathroom. I came out of the bathroom, and I saw him, so we started walking toward the front of the bar. I was holding his hand, trying to stay close to him, fighting through the crowd. He let go of my hand because someone pushed in between us. We kept walking forward toward the front door to get outside. He was in front of me, and once we were just outside the bar, I turned around just for a second, and BOOM... I didn't see him anymore! He was gone! I was looking all around, in front of me, behind me, on both sides — I didn't see him anymore. WTF was going on? I stopped where I was because he couldn't have gotten far, so I was looking around, hoping to spot him. But no, I was not seeing him. All I saw were lots and lots of people, and it seemed like more and more people kept coming and bumping into me.

I was trying not to panic, and I was telling my self to just stay calm, he couldn't have gotten far before realizing I wasn't with him... right? I'm not a panicky kind of person. It normally takes a lot to rattle me. I was thinking, just go right back inside the bar we just came out of, and maybe he went back inside. I went inside, looking everywhere, hoping to see him. Nope, no sign of him at all. Just lots and lots of people jammed packed everywhere like packed sardines. I walked back outside and decided to stay in that general area because I couldn't imagine he would just leave, and if I stayed there, he was bound to see me... right? Well, so far, NO!

Ok, I was standing on the side of the building still by the same bar, watching people walking by on the sidewalk, telling myself that I was going to see him any minute. I was looking at my watch, and from the time we got to the first bar, it was around 5 o'clock or so and when we left the bar it was about 8ish. It was about 9 p.m. now, and I was wandering the streets of Chicago. I was pacing and thinking to myself, what am I going to do? I was telling myself, ok, think think think about this. But there were just so many fucking people all around me, I couldn't think! Here was the situation: I left my purse in his car, so I had no phone, no money, and I didn't even have his address. Yeah, shits pretty fucked up right about now. More importantly, I didn't even know his phone number by heart! This is the age where no one does that anymore, you just put numbers in your cell phone. I have to say, I didn't see this one coming at all. Normally, I'm prepared and have already thought of all the different situations and scenarios that could possibly happen. But not this time. Who would ever think that a grown woman would get separated in a crowd of hundreds and hundreds of people on the streets of Chicago? I know, me neither.

Time was creeping by, and I was panicking! I had never felt this helpless before in my entire life, and just the thought

65

that I had no idea what to do or where to turn was starting to feel debilitating. I'd seen a few policemen patrolling the streets, but what would I have said, I have no information to give? He'd probably look at me like you dumbass, let me get this straight. You just met this guy online, you flew to Chicago, you're staying in his apartment, you don't know where that is, you don't have his phone number, and you left your purse in his car? Is that what you're telling me? Yeah, wasn't ready to go there just yet. I mean, I did have his name and the name of the company he worked for. But if I went there, then that would be the point of no return. And was I there yet? Right, so I left the police out of it. (I mean, my guy was completely harmless. I am not a naïve girl. I don't attract stalkers, so this was definitely not one of those predatory situations. Just wanted to clear that up.)

All I could do was walk the streets and hope to find him. I started walking down the street, I turned the corner, and still nothing. I was trying to remember where we parked and believe it or not, I found the car, but he wasn't there. I waited there for about 30 minutes or so then I decided to leave because I believed he was probably looking for me too.

By now, I was so tired, overwhelmed, and felt so defeated. I felt like a zombie, and I was trying to keep from shaking uncontrollably. Now I know how a child feels when they are lost in a store. These are not familiar feelings for me. My natural instinct is to never give up, there is always a solution to everything. But I was just exhausted right now, and I just needed to sit down and rest for a minute. I found a spot on the sidewalk against a wall and just fell to the floor, and I started to cry. Tears of frustration and fear started rolling down my face. I couldn't stop them from falling. A small group of people was walking toward me, and I heard someone say, "Are you ok?" All I could say was, "Yeah, I'm good." Mainly because I was so embarrassed about the crazy situation I was in. What was I going to say, help me find a light-skinned black man who left me outside of a bar and never came back? Nope couldn't do it.

After I got myself together, I got up and decided to retrace my steps. I headed back to the original bar we were last together. By that time, hours had gone by. As I was walking, I was praying that I found him soon because I didn't know how the hell I was going to get home, and that was all I wanted right about now just to be at home where I was out of this nightmare. And now I'm talking to myself. What the hell is wrong with you? Why are you even here, dummy? All this love shit is about to get you killed! Ok. Ok, pull yourself together, snap out of it. You are sounding crazy!

It was probably about midnight now, and I turned the corner and walked back toward the street where the bar was where we first got separated, and as I was walking and getting closer to the front door, Dion seemed to come out of nowhere and grabbed me and said, "OMG there you are!!!" I heard him say, "Where have you been? I've been looking all over for you." He looked more irritated than relieved. Huh. But then he saw my face. The deer in headlights look, along with confusion and on the verge of a complete breakdown. He grabbed me and hugged me, and all I could do was cry with relief. He asked me, "Where did you go? Why did you leave this area? And all I could muster up was, "I was here... I was here... I ... I..." then he just pulled me to him and held me to keep me from shaking. He started walking me toward his car, down the street and around a couple of corners, and nothing was said. When we finally got to his car, there was a note he'd left on the windshield. He said he left it in case I came to the car. But it must have been after I left because it sure wasn't there when I found the car. But that didn't matter anymore, nothing mattered. At this point, I was a total zombie, I was delirious, and I couldn't even speak. He was very comforting and handled me with extreme care because he knew how fragile I was at this point. I mean, I was totally traumatized, and I really wanted to go home.

See, told you, very EVENTFUL, right? It had started to thunder outside, and the thunder was loud. The rain and the loud thunder, it was all very fitting considering the traumatic night I'd just had. We got back to his place, and he put me in the bed. Very little was said until I finally fell asleep in his arms. He held me the whole night. I think he was afraid to let me go.

Yup, crazy, right? Yes, that actually did happen. The next day, I caught a flight and headed home. We never spoke of that night ever again.

Crazy enough, I still wanted to see him. So, I did. We talked on the phone and texted, and we planned my next trip there. I felt like that wasn't how I wanted to remember Chicago. The next month, I flew out to the Windy City once again. The weather was still good, more thunderstorms but still warm out, which I luv.

He picked me up on a Friday, and we headed to an outdoor concert he got us tickets for. He named a bunch of bands that I had never heard of, and then he said, "Snoop Dog!" I said, "Well, ok, of course, I'm in. Shit, that's fuckin SNOOP DOG!" We got there and we parked in this big dirt area that was half muddy half dry because apparently, it had been raining off and on all day. (Yes, of course, he picked me up in his shitty car so his good car wouldn't get damaged in the storm. You know, by water. Lol.)

We got there and hided on up to where the stage area was and fo und our seats. Not close at all to the stage but at least we could see... kinda. Next thing you know, yup, it started to sprinkle then rain. WTF, why are we still Outside? This was definitely some white shit. Oh, by the way, Dion is half black and half white hence all the white activities. Lol. Then the rain stopped, Snoop came on, and everyone lost their frickin minds! And yes, we had a blast! I know that was so white. Lol.

The next day he had planned for us to go to an outdoor cultural art festival. I really didn't know what to expect, but when we got there, it was very much a Black event. It was a shocker given how he was more on the white side, so I was pleasantly surprised by how interested he was in all the black art they had there.

On my last day there, we did some sightseeing, very tall buildings, amazing. He took me to lunch in one of the talles buildings in the world, I think. It's where they found Chris Farley, the comedian, dead in his hotel room. Remember that? Anyway, we had drinks on the top floor, or at least I think it was the top floor, it was very high up. Amazing view. We did a little roaming around and found a quiet spot to do a little kissing and touching, but then we heard someone coming, so headed for the elevator. While alone in the elevator, we started again with the kissing and touching. Boy, was I turned on right now. Of course, the we reached our floor and had to stop. Damn. Damn. Damn. Not too long after that, I caught a flight back home.

Alright, so let us talk a little sex, so I don't lose my readers. Some of our conversations had been of the sexual nature. What we liked, what we're into, things we had tried, and things we wanted to try. Things like that. So, of course, he said THREESOME! I know,

71

Surprise! Surprise! I told him I'd never been interested in a threesome.

"But why? You are so hot!" he said.

Like that's a criterion. SMDH. I told him I was more of a watcher, not really a participator. He asked me about things that I had tried, and my response was I'd only done the basics.

He laughed and said, "Well, I haven't done very much either." He asked me if I had a vibrator.

"Of course not. Oh, I mean, is this a serious question?"

"Yeah. I thought most women had one."

"Well, I don't, and I've never even seen one except on TV."

"Ok, just asking," he said.

The conversation went back to the threesome thing. I told him I was always curious about clubs like in that movie Eyes Wide Shut, you know, where people have sex, and you can watch.

"Oh, ok, yeah. I know what you're talking about," he said.

I asked him if he knew of any like that. He said, "No, but I can find some."

Honestly, I didn't really think much about it, but he certainly did because each time I talked to him after that, he gave me his search updates.

He e-mailed me a few links, and I looked them up, but when I saw one place, I was like WTF? I'm not going there. It was an old-fashioned-looking house from the 70s. I told him I needed something more modern, preferably with no wood paneling. Oh, and the people I saw looked just like the house, straight out of the 70s. Not good. We kinda got outta that whole sex club thing and then got on to swinging, which I didn't even know what that was. I told him I didn't think I was comfortable with being in a room full of people just going at it. "What about just one couple and us?" he suggested.

"I'm not watching you with another girl, so I don't know what to tell you," I said.

"Ok, I won't do that," Dion said.

"I'm not FUCKING another guy!" I almost screamed.

"Ok, ok, calm down. What about if we have a little fun with the girl?" he asked.

"Maybe. And if I say yes, I have to be ok with the couple, and there will be rules you must abide by."

"Ok, that's fine with me," he agreed.

I guess at this age—33ish—I felt like exploring a little... and so I did.

Over the next couple of weeks, he tried to

find suitable couples, and he became frustrated because he thought it would be easy to accomplish, but it was not. This was 2006ish, so the problem was that it wasn't as easy to find something like that. Back then, you couldn't just do a search and find good-looking couples who wanted to get together. I didn't do any of the looking. I left that up to him, but he wasn't really having any luck. I think it was because he obviously didn't care about the guy, he cared what the girl looked like because that was going to be his turn on, seeing her and us together. Well, finally, it was the weekend that I was coming to town. The next evening, he had a couple he was talking to that he set up for us to meet at a restaurant, so we could see if we wanted to go any further. Alright, so let's just get to it. It was Saturday night, and we headed to an agreed-upon restaurant at about 8 o'clock. We were there waiting and nothing. He called them, and I guess they said they were running late. Anyway, not too long after that, they showed up. She was black and about my age, and he was a white man about 10 years older. I didn't think he was attractive at all, but I was assuming Dion liked that fact. She was darker skin, thin, and ok, I guess. She was very outgoing because she did most of the talking.

We chit-chatted with each other, trying to get all the uncomfortableness out of the way, and we were trying to decide if we even wanted to go through with it. Ok, basically, it was me. Everyone was being EXTRA with me, basically trying to make me feel comfortable so they could get me naked and watch me FUCK! They were both looking at me like they wanted to eat me up.

Dion asked them if we could have a moment to talk. They left and went to another table, or outside, or I don't know where they went, but Dion asked me, "So, what do you think?" He had this stupid look on his face like a kid that was excited Santa Claus finally came to town.

"This is the best you could get? I commented to him.

"Yup. You should've seen the other ones," he answered.

We just laughed, and he tried to convince me that at least she was decent. I said, "Yeah, I guess she's pretty cool."

I thought about it, and in my head, I was thinking, ok, do you really want him around someone he's really attracted to that's gonna be naked? So I can then get mad and jealous, and then it turns into a murder cover-up, because I just killed the bitch for touching my man, and then he's gonna have to help me cover up this whole fucking thing since it was his idea?

Ok. Ok. Ok. I'm back.

"Well, I guess so," I finally said. Now we needed to decide on the location. "I'm not going to nobody's shitty hotel!" I announced. I was thinking, how do we know someone else won't be following us?

"Ok," Dion said. "Ok, right. Then why don't we just go to my place, and they can follow us from here?"

As if they couldn't call someone on their cell phone during the drive and tell them where they were going? Obviously, we didn't think this all the way through, but, oh well, we were already in it, so here we go. We headed back to his place but instead of it being just us like all the other times before, this time, we were on our way to a sexual escapade!

We got there, and we freshened up. I told him to remember our rules. "He's not touching me, and she's not touching you. Right?" Dion agreed. For the people in the back that aren't sure what's going on, basically, we are just watching each other have sex. Except that's not exactly what

76

happened.

I went into Dion's bedroom, and I changed into a fitted tank top and some booty shorts and came out into the living room, where apparently everyone was waiting on me. I saw the couple on one couch, and Dion was on the other couch. I knew they told me their names when we met at the restaurant, but I don't remember nothing. Let us just call our sex couple Keisha and Tom. Dion motioned for me to come to him, and I went over and sat next to him. He kissed me, slow and passionately and long. While Dion was kissing my neck, I turned my head to look at Keisha and Tom, and they were kissing too. She started moaning, and damn, they were really going at it. As I was kissing Dion, the next thing I knew, I suddenly felt another hand on my back. I opened my eyes, and it was Keisha. I don't really remember when my clothes left my body, but I was naked, and Keisha was really turned on because she kept complimenting my body. Ok, so at this time, I was 33, 5 feet 5 inches tall, and I weighed about 138 pounds. Dion kind of got on the carpeted floor, and I moved down with him, and we were still kissing and touching. Here comes Keisha, and she kind of started touching and rubbing my back, my arms, and then my breasts. She kept complimenting me as she started kissing the same areas. I think Dion sensed me about to pull away, so he started to kiss me and rub on me to try to comfort me so I didn't freak out. I knew it was really turning him on, and I knew that was his fantasy soooo, I let her.

I leaned back and gently pulled away from Dion and looked at him. He got up on the couch facing us, and Keisha started moving lower on my body, then she started going to town downtown. Dion was in heaven, so although I felt absolutely no pleasure at all (seriously not feeling anything), I figured I would give Dion his fantasy or the closest he was gonna get to it. Oh, and if you're wondering about old Tom, well, he was having a party all by himself on that side of the couch. On the other side of the couch, Dion was also going to town because I was putting on a show for him. I was moaning at all the right times because I think even Keisha thought she was doing a great job, but little did she know I FELT NOTHING (and I'm not just saying that, I really mean it.) Dion came down with us and tried to join in. I saw his hand on Keisha's back, and I reached around and pushed it down. Twice! (Follow the rules, Nigga! Damn!) I let her continue for, I don't know, 10 minutes or so, then that was enough. I gave one good cry cuz I guess that's when people think you're about to cum or orgasm or whatever you call it, right. Dion kind of came in and pounced on me and acted like Keisha wasn't even there. He started kissing me like an animal, and that was when I really got turned on, and then he entered me in all different positions until we both Climaxed! Pretty passionate and very, very HOT!

As we were lying there, trying to catch our breaths, we heard moaning. Then we realized we totally forgot that Keisha and old Tom were still here. We almost burst into laughter, but we kept it together because we didn't want to be rude. We just wanted them out. Since they kept on going, I whispered in Dion's ear, "Get rid of them."

I got up and went into the bedroom and closed the door behind me. After I went to the bathroom, I heard voices, so I hurried up and got in the bed and acted like I was falling asleep. The door opened, and I heard Keisha's voice.

"I just want to tell her goodbye," Keisha said.

I'm thinking, Bitch, why? This was not a love connection!

Dion, being the polite guy, said, "I think she's just really worn out. This has been quite a night for her."

But she came over to me anyway and sat next to me on the edge of the bed and said, "Hey, I just wanted to say goodnight and want to tell you that you are such a beautiful woman. If you ever need anything, you can call me."

Not sure what that meant, so I smiled and said, "Ok, thank you."

She leaned over and kissed me on the cheek and got up, and Dion walked them out. And that was that. We never really talked about anything like that again. That was the extent of my sexual adventurous side.

On another visit to Chicago, he had planned for us to go into the city and do some sightseeing. We got into his Corvette and drove to a parking lot because we were going to take the train since I'd never done that (not sure why he chose to drive his Corvette because we were only gonna park it and take the train... but whatever).

Let me say that I was excited to be in Chicago again. I'd never been on a train before. I know it may seem like no big deal to the rest of you, but I was there in Chicago with someone I was into. I was feeling pretty good right about now. I know what you're thinking, the train is dirty and not a glamorous means of transportation. You may be right about that, but for me, I was having a great experience being out of my norm, and I luved it!

We got to the city, and it was busy but not crazy. It was perfect. I saw all the tall buildings, and he was telling me what they all were. Dion was a pretty good tour guide. It was a nice day out, a little muggy and a little rainy, but it was warm and not cold, so it was nice to me. I would much rather be hot than cold. I was taking everything in, and it felt like I was in another world.

We found a spot to have lunch, and we enjoyed each other's company. There was some hand holding, some hugging, and kisses here and there. We did some more wandering, so now it was early evening, and he wanted to take me to have a drink in one of the skyscrapers so we could enjoy the view. And boy, what a view! I was feeling pretty high without actually being high, if you know what I mean. I hope you know what I mean.

I started thinking about the fact that I'd be going home soon, and I'd be getting back to reality. Isn't that the worst, when you are having such a good time then you think about leaving? What a downer. I tried to live in the moment, but reality reared its ugly head. He saw that my mood was shifting and said, "I know. I hate that you're leaving tomorrow. I wish you could just stay and never leave." That was a nice thought, and for that moment, that was enough.

The next time I saw Dion was when he finally came to Arizona. Of course, we continued to talk on a regular basis. But after about 6 months, I think I was starting to lose some steam. Not quite feeling the same connection, but I couldn't quite put my finger on it.

He got into town on a Saturday morning, and we hung out around my neighborhood because Sunday, I got us tickets to the Cardinals game. The more I was around Dion, the more I started to notice we really didn't have that much in common. He didn't really have a sense of humor because I had to keep explaining what I meant when I joked or kidded about something, so he didn't take it the wrong way, which was super annoying. He seemed to talk about himself a lot and all his interests. But when I talked about myself, he always managed to shift the conversation back to him. I was observing it all and seeing where it would lead.

It was Sunday, and we were getting ready to go to the Cardinals game. We headed out and made it to the stadium and dealt with parking, and finally made it inside to our seats. I noticed he seemed surprised I got such good seats. I told him before that I didn't like bad seats, or I'd rather watch it on TV. I knew what he was thinking. He was thinking about the shitty seats he got us at the baseball game back in Chicago. He knew those tickets were way cheaper than football game tickets. JS. He acted like it was no big deal when in fact, these tickets were a big fuckin deal. Nigga, I paid $200 for these tickets! Again. JS.

The game was over, and we headed out to find the car and try to navigate through the madness. He suggested that he drive, and I was ok with that. For some reason, he was driving like a total crazy person. He was driving so close to cars and very fast, and we were still in the parking lot! Ok, this was crazy because why would you drive like this in someone else's car? He did not drive like this in Chicago. Very weird, to say the least.

It was right around the six-month mark that we'd been dating. He had sent me flowers one time, and I'd flown out to Chicago to see him four times. Oh, and I flew to see him in California too, remember? I was starting to see that it was kind of getting to be one-sided, and I noticed that he was kind of on the cheap side as well. Not good. The reason I say that he was cheap is because one weekend, we met in Las Vegas when he had to be there on business for a week. I flew there only to give it, whatever this was, one last try. I will say I was not hopeful that it would end well.

It was a Friday, and it was Halloween. I got to Vegas, and Dion picked me up from the airport, and we headed to Caesars Palace, where he had been staying that past week. I walked into the hotel room, and on the desk, I saw all kinds of food laid out, like a 99 Cent store. I mean, there were bags of chips, cookies, pretty much any snack you can think of, it was there.

"Ok, I know you've been here a week, but damn, you're at a hotel, and there are places to eat around here." I guess he saw the look on my face.

"I know there's a lot here, huh?" he said. "Yeah, are you moving in?"

He laughed and said, "It's expensive eating out here in Vegas."

Ok, at that moment, I was thinking, WTF, who says that? "Aren't you working for a 'Fortune 500 Company' that you keep telling me about? But you can't afford to eat at restaurants here?" I just shook my head. Ok, whatever.

It was time to get ready for a night out. He said he found us a club to go to. I was excited about that. We got to the club, and it was pretty much all BLACK! Yessss!!! You know I was in heaven, right. Lol. We grabbed a couple of drinks and stood around, checking things out. You know what I mean — listening to the music, feeling the vibe. They were playing good music. I was getting into it, and so was Dion because when I looked at him, he was starting to bob his head, but I noticed that it was not really on beat. Hmmm. He looked at me and said, "Let's dance." He grabbed my hand and pulled me to the dance floor. It was a little crowded, so there was not a lot of room to move around, which was a good thing because this muthafucker started doing some weird shit. I mean, I don't even know how to describe it other than he was just moving all around. Kind of bouncing up and down, then side to side. I know it was not just me thinkng it was crazy because when I looked around, I saw a couple of guys standing in front of us. They first were looking at me, then I saw their eyes go in Dion's direction. Then they started to laugh and point at him.

Holy shit, this was fuckin' embarrassing. Why didn't I notice this before at the first club we went to back in Chicago? I don't know, but the more he felt the music, the more he started to move his body all over the place like he was possessed. Ok, I can't take it anymore. I told him I needed a drink, so we left the dance floor. I was so embarrassed. Damn, his White side decided to show up tonight. SMDH. A little while later, he asked me if I wanted to dance. It was a definite no for me. I just wanted to call it a night, and we did just that.

The next day, we hit the strip to try and find a show for that night. We walked to the Venetian and headed toward their box office to see what they had. We saw nothing we were interested in except Wayne Brady, the comedian. I was up for that. Shit, I needed a laugh right about now. I was standing off to the left while he was buying the tickets at the box office. Not sure what the hold-up was, but there was a line behind us. I turned to Dion, and I could hear him haggling with the box office guy.

"Come on, those aren't even good seats," I heard Dion say.

I just shook my head because, damn, just pay for the damn tickets. You can't make a deal every fuckin' time you buy something! He finally bought the tickets that were only $60 a ticket. This is what you were trying to get a deal on, $60 tickets? You know the look I had on my face, right?

We got outside in front of the hotel and as we were walking, to my left were the Gondola rides. You know the Venetian is the whole Italy theme, hence, the Gondola rides. I started walking slower to see if he was going to ask me if I wanted to go for a ride. You know, because it was romantic, and we were there together as a couple. We were almost about to pass them when I decided to say something.

"So, you're not going to ask me if I want to take a Gondola ride?"

He stopped and said, "You know, I thought about it. Do you know how much they are?"

"Probably no more than $30," I said.

"Yeah, I thought about it, but I just spent all this money on the tickets for tonight."

You mean the whopping $120.00? That money? Un-Fuckin-Believable! Ok, let me just get the fuck out of here before I push him in front of traffic.

It was about 8 o'clock, so we headed out for the

night. We decided to walk since the Venetian was not very far from our hotel. We got to our seats, which weren't the worst but not the greatest either. Remember, $60. You definitely get what you pay for. To our delight, Wayne Brady was pretty funny. I liked the show. I had a good time and laughed a lot. Damn, I needed that laugh.

After the show, we got outside, and as we started walking, it started drizzling. Just a light drizzle, so don't worry, I didn't run for cover. Cuz you know the hair thing. I am Black. Lol. As we were stopped, waiting at the crosswalk, I felt the cold air hit me. I crossed my arms, you know, because I was COLD. I could see Dion in the corner of my eye looking at me. Fellas, what would you do as you're walking with your lady outside in the cold rain? Being the gentlemen that you guys are, I know what you would say. But unfortunately, Dion would not agree with any of you. Oh, did I mention I had a short sleeve dress on? Dion, instead of giving me the blazer he had on, put his arms around me and rubbed my shoulders for a quick second, then proceeded to walk ahead when the light turned green. Yup, that was what he did. I know, a true gentleman. I was so done with this muthafucker.

The next morning, he got me to the airport and said, "Please let me know when you get home safely." I just nodded my head and was happy to be leaving. Once I got home safe and sound, I called Dion. Not even sure why I did, but I guess I wanted to see what he had to say to me, which was a whole lot of nothing, just like I thought.

The first thing this muthafucker told me was how mad he was because he bet on some game and lost $500.00. Ain't that some shit? That's when I knew I was so right about him. Basically, if he didn't want to spend money on something, he wasn't. And not because he didn't have the money. See, I told you he was a cheap and selfish man. What a damn shame.

From being around Dion, I noticed that we were always doing what he wanted to do. I mean, he would ask me what I wanted to do, then he gave me some options, but then he picked what he wanted, not what I chose. Hmmm... For example: We were sightseeing in downtown Chicago. I wanted to go one way, and he explained why we were going the other way. We were hungry, so he asked me what I had a taste for? He gave some suggestions, and I said, "how about seafood?" He said, "how about a chicken salad?" Okaaay...Then I thought, WTF did you even ask me for? When we were walking, he would kind of forget I was walking with him. He had a fast walk, so he started getting ahead of me. Then he would realize that I was not next to him anymore, and then he'd slow down. WTF! Who does that? That's probably why we were lost for 5 hours that time I was in Chicago.

I mean, I think in the beginning you don't really see or notice anything because you are caught up in the newness of a relationship and the fantasy of finding someone and having a happy ending and blah blah blah. But as time goes on, the nice, thoughtful guy you had in the very beginning soon disappears, and the real guy shows up. Your eyes start to open. And for me, that means I will start to look at you differently. In most cases, I will start to see who you really are and what you really look like because he was bound to show up eventually. And that is because you can't just turn into someone you're not and keep that up for very long. And when I start to see the real you, I start to realize that on top of you being an asshole, you don't even look that good at all. And I'm like, "Who the Fuck is this guy? This is the guy I've been seeing all this time? Damn, you are UGLY!" Ok, I'm done. I'm not dealing with a selfish, no sense of humor having, Ugly man! And so, after 6 months, that was the end of Dion.

CHAPTER FIVE: SOUTHERN CALIFORNIA

Alright, here goes another BPM date—Anthony from California, where I am from.

We started messaging each other, and then we exchanged numbers, then came the calls. Conversations were good, and we spoke often, so then we needed to meet. I believe that communication without meeting can be a waste of time, mainly because you invest all that time and don't know if you will even have a connection. Ok, look, I've been on dates where he looked pretty good in his pictures, but when we met, not so much. It's not that it wasn't him or a catfish, nothing like that. It's just that sometimes pictures don't translate well in person. Remember the "You look worse than your pictures?" Well, that's a real thing. I would rather meet sooner than later, so no one gets their time wasted.

I volunteered to come out to Cali for a

weekend, so we could meet, and since I was in Arizona, it wasn't a big deal for me to drive out. So, I did just that.

I got to the restaurant where we agreed to meet, and I was seated at a table. I texted him, "I'm here and at a table." A few more minutes went by, so I ordered a drink, a Mai Tai. I was sitting at a table facing the door, so I could see people coming in and out. It was about 3 o'clock, so it wasn't very crowded yet. I saw a few people come in until I saw a man that fit Anthony's description. He was tall, 6'3". I don't know anything about weight, but his weight fit his height. Whew. He was light-skinned and had green eyes. I saw him look over at me and smile and it looked like this was my guy. We hugged and exchanged pleasantries. You know, like two people trying to act like it was no big deal; you know, stupid dating shit. Lol. He asked me how the drive was. I said it was pretty good — didn't hit much traffic, which was great for a Friday. Then he said, "I have to say, you are gorgeous, even better than your pictures." I thanked him, and I said, "I am relieved that you actually look like your pictures and not like a totally different person."

You're probably wondering, well, did you

like him or not??? And the answer is, "YES," I was attracted to him, so I was very happy about that. That was the first and most important step for me in order to move forward. He ordered a beer, and we also ordered food and started general conversation to break the ice and loosen up.

This is the part I hate about dating, the awkwardness where you're trying to feel each other out to see if you both feel the same. Ok, I have to say this, this is the part when the guy usually puts his best foot forward and is EXTRA about himself and how he treats me. I totally get it. You are trying to make a good impression. However, the part I don't like is that your first impression is not supposed to be so different from what you are normally like, that over time, this first impression person fades away and disappears, and this person I'm left with is nothing like that. And just how that first impression guy fades away, so do my feelings/interest. Why don't they get that?

Ok, you're probably saying, what about you? Don't you try to make a good first impression, too? And the answer to that is, "Uhhh, No!" The reason I say that is I am the same no matter who I meet. And since you don't know me, you probably think, yeah, right, lady. Well, you can ask anyone who knows me, and any guy I've dated or met, they will say, "yeah, she's always been the same since day one." I am not saying I'm perfect. I am just saying, you're not gonna meet a different person the more time passes. I am serious at the right times, I like to joke and talk shit, but I am never going to be rude or disrespectful to anyone. And I just luv to laugh. I generally like to have a good time. I am not going to act like I like you when I really don't. The more time passes, if we are really vibing, I will treat you even better. I look forward to that. Ok, with that being said, let us get back to my date.

I could see that Anthony was social and charming. He liked to talk and initiate conversations, which was great. There was a little bit of silence going on here and there, so he said, "You know what, why don't we get our first kiss out of the way right now, so we can move forward?" I looked at him, and then I smiled because that was pretty clever, and I luv a man who takes charge. Not the "I said come here, Bitch, don't move," kind of take charge. A man who leads, that's a turn on. I smiled and said, "Ok, that is actually a good idea." We kissed right there at the table. I mean, it wasn't a tongue down my throat kinda thing, so calm down, people. It was a nice slow, and short kiss. The kind that left you wanting more. So, ok, ok, I had to admit that was pretty smooth. I was all for moving forward. And we did. He showed me a great time in Cali, so I'm thinking we just might have something here.

I decided to head on out to Cali for another visit, but this time we were going to San Diego. I was supposed to meet Anthony at some address he gave me. Not sure where it was, but I was meeting him there. It was an address close to a military base. He was in the military part-time. I got there, and he got out of a big ole beat up green Chevy Camaro and not the Chevy Impala I last saw him in. Basically, the last car he was driving was a rental the weekend we first met. I'm not just saying that to talk shit or be mean. It was a big green machine. That spit out smoke. I think that's what he called it, and he said, and I quote, "I can't have you ride in this car, you definitely don't belong in something like this." See, it was not just me.

Thank goodness I drove my car. At that time, I had a Mercedes C Class. Not a big deal, but compared to that thing, it surely was. We parked his green machine somewhere I didn't really care where only that it was far away from me. Ok, so he made plans for us to meet up with his friends at a park in San Diego. They were having a little gathering — food, drinks, volleyball, and some game where you hit a ball that looked like a pool ball except a little bigger with a stick to try and see who could hit it the farthest. Yes, these were white folks. Lol.

We got there, and he introduced me to everyone, about 7 or 8 people, and they were very nice and friendly. No kind of weirdness or bad vibes at all. About half of them were playing volleyball, and 3 or 4 ladies had me sit with them on the sidelines. Of course, they started grilling me with questions about how we met, where I was from, what I thought about him, etc. You know, the basic nosy friends' questions. But I didn't mind because they meant well, and they were very friendly and inviting toward me. I answered all their questions and told them that I liked Anthony and things were very new but going very well so far. A few minutes later, after almost busting his ass trying to dive for balls, Anthony joined us. He was pretty affectionate, kisses on the cheek, hugs, hand holding, pretty much what girls like. It was all covered.

After being there for about 3 hours, it was

getting chilly, so I was ready to go. We headed to the Gaslamp Quarter and found a restaurant/bar to have dinner. I had an ok time, only because I'm not a bar kinda gal, but if I were, I would have loved that area.

The next day, he had San Diego Charger tickets. By the way, in case you hadn't noticed, I luv sports, tennis, basketball, football, and in that order.

It was a packed stadium, so I was a little nervous given the horrible nightmare I had in Chicago not too long ago. But I was ok. I don't let things like that stop me from doing anything. It was in the past, I'm with a different person, and I definitely wouldn't put myself in the same situation again. It was halftime and we got up to grab some food and use the bathroom. Before we parted ways, I told him, "COME RIGHT BACK HERE AFTER YOU'RE DONE. I CAN'T GET LOST!" I wanted to make sure he got the point. I used the bathroom, and I found Anthony pretty easily because he was actually paying attention and made sure I saw him. As I walked toward him, he then suddenly grabbed me, bent me over, and kissed me. You know, like in the old movies when a couple hasn't seen each other in a long time, and they are finally reunited. They run to each other, then he takes her in his arms, bends her over, and kisses her like they are the only two people in the world. Yup, like that. He was scoring a lot of points here... Yes, he was.

I came down for another weekend, and that weekend I was finding out more and more about ole Anthony and his everyday life. I was wondering how many of you, when you first start dating someone, do you have to say, "I live alone" or is that a given? You know us being grown and all. I am 34 and you are 35, and I really didn't think I needed to ask if you lived alone. We both have children, and I just thought that that was a given. You know, I'm divorced, so I live alone. Right. A given. Welp, I am wrong again. Damn.

On this visit, I found out that Anthony, a 35-year-old man, lived with his parents in their townhouse in Orange County. It was not a big townhouse either. I guess the only reason I found this out was that we went by there because he had to do something for them. The really crazy part was that this was absolutely no big deal to him. I mean, he acted like this was totally normal. Totally acceptable for a grown ass man with children ... Bleep... Bleep... Bleep!!! THIS IS TOTALLY NOT!!! I met his parents, and they were nice people and totally loved me. I think they were happier that he was dating someone that was well put together. Kind of wondering what he had dated before. Maybe they were trying to get him out of their house, which I totally didn't blame them. Damn, how much longer are you planning to stay there? I mean, do you have a plan or what? This revelation just did not sit well with me. I was in the living room with his mother, chit-chatting, and I could hear Anthony and his dad in the kitchen. I heard his dad say, "Anthony, you guys are not staying here. Get a room for that girl. Stop being cheap." At this point, I was looking like, WTF. He was actually thinking about staying there? He certainly did not mention that to me. Before I could say anything about it, he took his dad's advice and booked a room for us. I'm sure you know the look on my face... definitely not smiling.

This is where you start questioning what else don't you know about this guy because this is crazy. I mean, stability is my middle name. Always has been. Unfortunately, this is where we get into trouble. You know, when you have already invested time and are developing feelings. Then you start getting little red flags, but because of how you're feeling, you tell yourself it's not a big deal.

You come up with reasons why it's not a big deal and just ignore them. Well, people, I am here to tell you what you already know. These red flags, no matter how small, are a big deal, and they are not going to go away. They are warnings of what is sure to come. And that is DISASTER!!! So please, don't ignore them. Address them right then and there. Take my word, it will not get better if you don't. One of these days, I'm gonna take my own damn advice. Ok, that's it. I'm done preaching... for now. You are probably wondering why I was the one traveling to Cali for us to see each other. Well, first of all, I like driving. Any chance I get to go back to Cali, I take. It's about 5 hours, and during that time, I have my music and my thoughts, so it goes by pretty fast for me. Second, I have every other weekend free, so I would rather go to Cali than stay in Arizona because Cali is the SHIT!!! Honestly, I really don't mind being the one to travel.

That being said, it seems to me that if I'm your "girl," and I'm using air quotes and using that word very loosely, wouldn't you be offering some gas money? Or even offer to fly me there. Damn. Nope, not one time. SMH...Just saying. I don't know what it is about me that men don't offer these things. I

, guess they see me and see someone well put together, that has her shit together, and I guess they don't think I could use some gas money, flowers, perfume, candy, sunflower seeds, shit ANYTHING. I mean, last time I checked, gas was not free. I don't know if it is pure oblivion, cheapness, or they can't afford it. I would definitely like to know the answer to this.

Anyway, we were still talking in between visits and still getting along, so we decided to plan a weekend to San Francisco. He was actually from the Bay area, excuse me, the "Yay area." Ok, that weekend arrived, and I hopped a flight to Frisco. Anthony met me there. Oh, the reason for this trip was that it was his 10-year high school reunion. I know, fun times.

I landed in Frisco, and he picked me up from the airport. We headed to have dinner and drinks with some of his friends. I don't really remember what part of town we were in, but we got to a nice little restaurant, cool hip spot. (I've been told that no one says hip anymore, and it shows how old you are...but ask me if I care). We joined his friends at a table outside and had a good time. Pretty good vibes. It was nice getting to know new people and hearing stories about how they were back in the day. It was late, so we headed back to our hotel and got ready for the next day.

Ok, I know what you're thinking. So, you guys just went to sleep? What's happening in that hotel room? ...Ok, ok, ok, you know what happened. Yes, we had some grown folks relations... some good ole, grown folk relations, and I'm not gonna give you guys all the damn details! Damn! Y'all Nasty! Lol

So, like I was saying, it was the next day, and we met up with more of his friends, and we had plans to go to a jazz festival in this very big place. It was outdoors, the Greek Theatre at the University of California, Berkley campus. It was huge. It was just us and one other couple. Apparently, Anthony and this guy had known each other for many, many years, and his girlfriend he brought had not been dating very long either, just like us. She was cool. We got along and had a pretty great time. During that time, I noticed some looks I was getting from his friend. Not anything uncomfortable, just glances. You know the ones you get when someone likes you, those kind. But he was pretty harmless, so no big deal. It was nothing new to me. It was the kinda shit that always seemed to happen to me. Most of the time, they didn't act on them, so it was harmless.

After the jazz festival, we headed back to the hotel to get ready for his high school reunion. I got this cute little colorful dress for the occasion, and Anthony just brought black pants and a dress shirt with his old looking leather jacket. You know, just basic shit. Something that he barely put any thought into. I noticed that it seemed to be his wardrobe personality. You know, any old shirt and jeans, or the same old black dress shirt if we went out anywhere that required a little more effort. Maybe he had more than one black shirt... shit, I hoped so. That dress personality was not coinciding with mine. I care what I look like and go shopping to update my wardrobe. You know, like a regular human being.

Cracks were starting to surface as more time went by. We got dressed and were ready to head out. He complimented me because I did look pretty fly. And I said, "you look good too." Oh, this time, his dress shirt was a powder blue. Thank the Lord, he bought a new shirt for the occasion. Ok, now I sound mean for saying what I said about him, right? Nope, it's the truth. One time does not make it a pattern.

We got to a hotel where the reunion was being held, spotted his friends, and walked in with them. It was a pretty good turnout, about 50 people or so. Music was mostly on the white side. I prefer more R&B and Hip Hop remember. We were standing around talking, kind of a club vibe now. They finally played a good song, and I wanted to dance. Apparently, Anthony did not dance. I know, what the hell. And I say, "At all?"

"Not really," he said.

One of his friends said, "I'll dance with you." I said, "Ok, cool." This was another one of his friends but this one was looking at me like he wanted to eat me up, and this one was married. Damn, I just wanted to dance, that was it. He kept complimenting me, and finally, the song was over. I spotted Anthony and headed over there. I saw that he was talking to his other friend's girlfriend. The one we went to the jazz festival with. I was getting a little weird vibe the closer I got, and I didn't see his friend anywhere. They saw me and acted a little weird, you know, like you were caught doing something you weren't supposed to be doing. I just looked at him, but I didn't say a word. I am not the confrontational type at all. Mainly, I just observe and let you hang yourself. And unfortunately, they always do. He said, "A bunch of us are going over to so and so's house, you want to go?" I said, "Sure."

Ok, now my mood has totally shifted to annoyed. That means I'm quiet and have short answers. Anthony was now being kinda extra; and what I mean by that is he is being extra attentive now, more hand holding, more hugging. You know, extra. I was just trying to figure out why he was acting like I didn't see the difference. Everybody knows the reason you act like this is that you are feeling guilty about something. Right. But you know what? I was gonna go with it and milk this fucking cow dry. He asked me if I was ok, and I said, "I'm fine. So, where are your friends? You know, the one you were being extra nice to?"

He just looked at me with this dumb look on his face and said, "What? Huh? I don't know what you're talking about." I just looked at him and said, "Right." Now let me tell you what's going to happen. He was going to be extra, extra, extra all night, and I was totally ok with that. I am going to see how far he is going to go with this situation.

We got to the friend's house where they were having a little house party. I guess they planned to have it the same night as the reunion. There was music playing and a lot of drinking going on, which was fine, however, beer is not my thing, and that was all they seemed to have. Anthony grabbed a beer and chit-chatted a bit with different people, but then he looked at me and saw this was not my thing. After about an hour he said, "Ok, let's go."

On the way back to the hotel, we were driving, and he pulled over on some road. We got out and walked to a cliff overlooking the city. It was quite beautiful. Amazing view. However, at this moment, I was not feeling any of it because he planted the bad seed at the reunion, remember?

Ok, I feel like half of you agree with me, and half of you are probably saying, you're making a big deal out of nothing. Right? Well, that may be the case, but I feel like if it was no big deal, and it was nothing, why was he going out of his way to smooth things over? That's all I'm saying.

I told him I was cold, so then we left. Maybe I over-exaggerated just a tad bit. In case I did, we made up once we got to the hotel. If you know what I mean, and I know you do.

The next day was when we were set to leave San Francisco. He goes back to Orange

County, and me back to Arizona. Our flights weren't until that evening, so we had some time to kill. He asked me if I wanted to meet up with Tony and ole Lisa? I said, "Ok, why not?"

Why not, you ask? Especially since there may or may not have been something going on there with Anthony and Lisa the previous night? Well, my thinking was I kinda wanted to see if there was anything there. So, I knew how to proceed. It was not that I was insecure, because I was not. It was that I needed to know if I could trust this man, so I needed to see how he interacted with someone I believed he might be attracted to. See, I cannot be with someone I can't trust or if I even question his loyalty. That is one thing that I will never overlook. So, yes, we met up with Tony and Lisa.

We got to a bar with not very many people there at all, which was cool. We had drinks, and there was a pool table in the back, so we started up a friendly game of couples' pool. Again, Anthony was still acting a little extra, and I realized maybe this was how he acted when he was around a pretty girl. The problem was not that he was acknowledging that she was pretty, it was the fact that it was his friend's girl, and if I was noticing it, I was pretty sure everyone else was too. The thing that was irritating to me was that I can control myself when other men are attracted to me (umm, which is pretty often), especially if I am with someone, so why aren't you? SMH. Because, trust me, your little feelings would have been crushed if I acknowledged every muthafucker that took notice of me! I'm Just Saying. But you know what... Fuck it! You wanna play this game? Ok, let's play!

Anthony went to get another round of drinks, and Lisa went to the bathroom, so that left Tony and me to have a conversation. BTW, I told you I got the "I like you" vibe from him on several different occasions since we'd met. We chit-chatted a lot about nothing, but the difference now was that I was open to some mild flirting. So, that is what we were doing. The part that irritated me again is that these two guys had been friends since high school. I would never, and have never, flirted with any of my friend's boyfriends. I was starting to think maybe they had done this before and maybe they were in competition with each other. Either way, I didn't really care at this point because I was trying to see how far it would go. There was some laughing between us, some brushing up against each other... you know, flirting.

While this was happening, I was making sure Anthony got glimpses of all of it. I know, you're probably saying you are kind of foul for this. Well, I say not really. Guys do this shit all the time. Anyway, it was working because Anthony hurried up to get back to me and started with the hugging and kissing on the cheek and in my ear right in front of Tony.

You're probably wondering where Lisa was because so was I. Before I could ask about her, here she came. It was back to four. Even though she was back, the guys weren't really paying her any attention. All eyes were on me. I mean, honestly, that wasn't what I wanted to happen, so blame it on Anthony, but that was what it was. Poor girl. I kind of felt bad for her. But it's not my fault your man ain't shit. I'm just trying to teach Anthony a lesson; is it my fault that I'm a good teacher.

After a few hours passed, I got a little hungry, so the guys went to the bar to order us food. This was a good opportunity for us girls to talk. Well, she kind of did all the talking because, frankly, I didn't really have much to say to her. I mean, she seemed like a nice person, but she was not my friend, and she'd already proven to be

110

untrustworthy, especially since she was flirting with my man. She started asking me how long Anthony and I had been dating, how it was going, and if I liked him. She said, "He really likes you." Bitch, I know. You don't have to tell me. Ok, Ok, sorry. I got caught up in the moment. Lol. But all I said was, "Oh really." I told you I didn't have much to say to her. But since she was all up in my face, I told her, "Yes, things are going well with us; but we'll see."

The fellas got back to us. Anthony came behind me, hugged me and walked me away from them to have a moment alone. He was in my ear, telling me how much he liked me. How much he was going to miss me and that maybe I should change my flight to stay longer. Oh, that's right, he was not leaving until the next day. But I said, "I would, but I have work tomorrow." Yup, blame it on work to get out of it. As Anthony was hugging me, from the corner of my eye I could see Tony looking at us. See, I told you, your man ain't shit. SMH. Ok, it was time to go, so we all said our goodbyes, how we should get together again soon, you know, all the fake shit; then I hopped a plane back home.

Another weekend I headed out to Cali for another visit. On this visit, Anthony talked about buying a car. You know, because his was a piece of shit that barely ran. Well, thank the Lord for that, because I can't be the only one driving all the time. You know you try not to be negative, but come on, why does anyone need to point out the obvious. Negro, you are in your mid-30s, you have kids, and you don't have a good running car. Well, I was glad I didn't have to say anything.

He wanted to go look at a couple of cars he found, which was fine. Even though maybe you should have taken care of this shit before I came. You know, so we can spend quality time together. But I'm ok with it because this is everyday stuff, and this is how you get to know if you can be around a person long term.

We got to the Mercedes dealership, and all I could say was ok, he's getting a Benz. I mean, I was happy he was, but I was also thinking can he really afford one? I mean, I'm glad I'm rubbing off on him, but let's be realistic about this. But then again, he should be able to because, shit, he lives with his parents. Once we looked at the ones he liked, he said, "I'll have to come back tomorrow because my dad is going to co-sign to help me get it. OMFG... this means Oh My Fuckin God! That's all I could think. The even more disturbing part was not that this was a 35-year-old man that needed his father to help him buy a car and couldn't buy his own shit. Nope, that was not the most disturbing part. The worst part about it was how he felt so comfortable saying this to me and had no shame in saying it out loud. I would have more respect for you if you just did this on your own and didn't tell me that you need your dad to buy a car.

I hate to put all his business out in these streets, but it's important for you to know about all these red flags that I continuously ignored. Please, don't ignore yours. These last couple of red flags told me about his true character. I get sometimes we need help because life throws you a curveball, and there's nothing wrong with accepting help while you're down. However, he'd been divorced for years, and he still lived with his parents and was using them to buy a car instead of handling his business on his own or until he could. That says a lot. But apparently, it didn't say enough because I was still with him. Lol!

Now it was getting close to Christmas, so even though I was having doubts about how far we were really going to go, I was moving forward. The reason why I say that, well, you know, you've read all my reasons. But I was willing to give him the benefit of the doubt, and I was hoping for the best. I suggested that he come to the AZ and spend Christmas out here. He accepted my invitation since he wouldn't have his kids this year. This year, I planned on cooking, and my sister and her family were coming over. Yup, nosy sis was trying to meet the new guy so she could see for herself if he was gonna make it or not.

Anthony flew in on Christmas Eve. I picked him up from the airport, and I was happy to see him. Also, happy because it seemed like forever since I had some "Special Attention," if you know what I mean. I know, I know. I'm nasty. Well, at least I'm trying to be. The plan was we would go have drinks with my sister and her husband but wouldn't stay out too late. I got a call from my sister, and she told me there was a change of plans. "We're going bowling instead of a bar." Ok, cool, couples bowling.

Alright, everyone was getting along, which was great. It was a fun night for everyone. Anthony was a hit, but I was the one who stole the show. We decided to bowl one more game, and guess who kept bowling strikes? Yup... ME! Don't ask me how, but I bowled about 9 strikes in a row. Guess who won?

Yup ME! Definitely beginner's luck, but I'll take it. Boy, I was feeling frisky now, so I was ret to go. Lol. It was Christmas day, and I got Anthony some presents. You know, it being Christmas and all.

I found out his sizes and got him clothes. I know what you're thinking. Are you trying to give some subtle hints about his wardrobe? And "YES," I was. I definitely was. Did I care if he was offended in any way? Nope. No, I did not. I mean, come on. You can't keep wearing the same shit every time I see you. It's not even that often. So, yes, I got him clothes. Like four outfits. Do you say outfits when referring to men? I don't know, but that's what it is. Oh, and a watch. Now I know you are wondering what did ole Anthony get me? Ok, let's get this straight. I did not buy him gifts just so he would get me something. I am not that person at all. I really just wanted him to look good. With that being said, Anthony, the man I'd been seeing for 5 or 6 months, who came to spend Christmas with my family and me, got me a CARD! Yup, a lonely ole card. WTF!!! Not even a bottle of wine to go with it or chocolates or a Twizzler. Nothing. Talking through a bull horn... "YOU HEARD ME, RIGHT? NOTHING ELSE, GUYS!"

I thought, more than anything, it was embarrassing because my sister would be here shortly, and she and her husband would want to know the answer to the same question. Again, I didn't expect a ring or anything, although he was always telling me that he wanted us to be together forever, and we should get married. Ok, maybe I did think he would get me some piece of jewelry. I am just saying, come on, you know this is some Nigga shit right here. Now, I was in a not so good mood.

My sister arrived, and we went to my room, and of course, she asked me. "Well, what did he get you?" And I said, "A card," with this look on my face. You know the kind when you want to cuss someone out, but you really can't because then you'll sound crazy. I mean, what would I have said? "Umm, Negro, where's my gift for real, because I know this damn piece of paper, ain't it?" See, that sounds crazy. Right about now, I was just trying to let it go and enjoy my Christmas. So, I did just that.

Alright, I am not going to lie to you about how I was feeling about Anthony and our relationship. When we'd talked about the future, he'd always made it clear that he wasn't moving anywhere until his kids graduated from high school. And that wasn't for at least five years. I didn't have a problem with that. I got it. But what rubbed me the wrong way was the way he said it. Like, sorry, Bitch, I don't know what to tell you. I'm not doing shit until I'm done with my kids. And I was thinking to myself, so you're just gonna stay with your parents until then? You're not even trying to get your own place. That's what was going through my mind. Did I really want to give this man five years of my life and maybe get thrown another curveball? Because he definitely was not looking like a stable guy right about now. Especially since I'd already invested six months into him and had not seen one thing that would indicate to me that we would have a good, stable, happy life together. The only thing that he had done was buy half a car. I don't even know if that counts.

After he left with a lot more stuff than he came with, I was distant and didn't have much to say. My birthday was coming up in a few days, and he said he had something planned. All I could say was, "I'm listening." I felt like he fuckin' knew he was on his last leg, so he was trying to get both legs back. He said, "Why don't we go to San Francisco for your birthday and for New Years?" We'll go to a Raider's game. I have a buddy who works for the Raider's, and he can get us tickets. We'll celebrate your birthday and New Year's out in Frisco." I thought, Ok, he's actually thought about it, and this sounds like it should be a good time. I said, "Yes, let's do it." A few days later, he asked me if I wanted to drive down to Cali, and we could all drive to Frisco together. Wait a minute. "Who's all?" He said, "Oh, I'm bringing my kids since I have them for New Year's."

You know what I was thinking, right? Here we fuckin' go with the surprises. Why didn't you say that when we first talked about this? Excuse me, why would I want to spend my birthday and New Year's with YOUR bad ass kids and not my own? I took a minute to calm down and think. It was already too late to change the plans. I'd already bought my ticket, so fuck it, I just went. I told him, "No, I will meet you there. I already have my ticket. He said, "Ok. We are going to have a great time!" I really hoped so.

Alright, here we go... It was my birthday! The big 35! I was feeling good and ready to have a great day. I caught a quick flight to Frisco and got scooped up by Anthony and his crew as soon as I landed. He timed it perfectly. He pulled up in some old van. He said it was his buddy's van. You know what, I really didn't give a shit. It was a running car. I greeted the kids and got in, and we headed to his people's house. He was dropping his kids off, and then we were going to get my birthday started. Or so I thought.

We got back in the van, and HE ASKED ME, "So, what do you want to do?" He saw the confused/disgusted look on my face and then said, "Ok, let's get something to eat, then we can decide." I just said, "Ok." We drove to some restaurant, nothing fancy at all. It was a restaurant equivalent to an Applebee's. Not that there's anything wrong with Applebee's, I'm just saying, IT'S MY FUCKIN' BIRTHDAY TODAY!!!!! Nigga, you lucky I'm starving. We ordered, we ate, and then we were sitting, waiting for the check. All I could think was, you have got to be kidding me. This is it? This muthafucker don't have NOTHING planned?!?! He asked me again, "So, what do you want to do?" I said, "Anthony, how would I know? I'm not from out here, you are. And you're asking me?" He paid and said, "Ok, let's go."

The reality of the situation had set in, and I was feeling the anger starting to bubble up inside of me. That's never a good sign. We pulled up back at his cousin's house, and we just sat there.

"You mean to tell me you didn't have anything planned for me today? I mean absolutely nothing?" I asked.

He had this stupid look on his face and said, "Well, I don't want to go in there if you're going to be acting like this."

I know what you're thinking... Oh no, he didn't! Yup, he did. That's when I let his sorry ass totally have it. I finished with, "All I got was a sorry ass meal for my birthday from you! I really just want to go home because this is not at all what I expected. It's nothing."

I guess at that point, he was thinking if he didn't start saying something, he was over. In his attempt to calm me down, he said he was sorry, he planned it all wrong.

"But we're going to have a great New Year's Eve and New Year's, so please don't go. I really am sorry I ruined your birthday."

"Fine, where are we sleeping tonight? Let's just go there."

Alright, I know what you're thinking... so what happened when you got to wherever you guys were going to lay your heads? The answer to that is nothing. I took my ass to bed and to sleep. Wasn't nobody putting on Jeremih "Birthday Sex." Nope, not this year anyway.

However, the morning, now that was a different story. I mean, shit, I had calmed down, and you know what the morning mood brings. What is it about that early in the morning time that just makes you so horny? You know what I mean. And since I know you do, you know what was happening in that bedroom at 6:30 a.m. Ok, now that we have gotten that out of the way, we can start our day.

It was New Year's Eve, and the plan was to pick up his kids and meet up with everyone at Raider's Stadium. Yup, his friends, kids — everybody. Some of these friends were new friends I had never met, mostly guys who came down for the game. Actually, they were all guys. I was the only female.

We got to his cousin's house to pick up the kids, and they were not ready yet, so we waited in the car. As we were waiting, he found a pair of full-size scissors. A big orange pair. You know the kind your teacher had in school, that size. I was looking at him, and he was looking in the rearview mirror, and then he proceeded to put them in his nose and was trying to trim his nose hairs. Talking about, "these bad boys are out of control." I was so disgusted that this nasty muthafucker saw nothing wrong with doing this in front of me. Before I could voice my disgust, here come the kids. They jumped in, he pulled off, and I was just shaking my head. That was some trifling shit right there. Then I had to put on a friendly face, knowing that nothing was off-limits with this guy.

Anyway, we got to the stadium as the tailgate was ending. We walked up, and there were probably 6 or 7 of us and his 3 kids. Alright, now I have to talk about his kids for a minute, just so you know what I was dealing with and why I called them "bad ass kids." I met them one weekend in Cali, and I expected them to be regular ole teenagers because their ages were 13, 15, and 16. Well, I was wrong. I'm sorry, but these are crazy little Chuckies, only they were not little. Let me explain.

We were out in Orange County, and we all went to a restaurant together. When we got there, they were all over the place, running around like little kids and loud. All Anthony would say, from time to time, was, "All right guys, settle down." We got into an elevator to get to the restaurant on the fifth floor, and these little bastards (that weren't little) started pressing every damn button, so it

122

kept stopping on every damn floor. I was standing there with this look on my face like WTF is going on? Anthony, on the other hand, was standing there looking like this was totally normal.

We finally made it to our floor, made it over to the restaurant, and got seated. We ordered, and during conversation, one of them got loud and said, "You're stupid, Dad, shut up." Anthony said nothing. During more conversations, there were a few more shut ups and stupids, oh, and no dummy, all directed at their dad. Ok, Ok, Ok, I know they were not my kids, but that was some white shit right there. I don't know one black person who would be ok with that whole fucked up situation. You know what, I didn't say anything because I wanted to see how far the Chuckies actually would go. I had a feeling it might be a little further. We finished our dinner and headed back downstairs, and there was a bar that we found. He told the kids that's where we'd be. They took off. I thought they must have been there before because they knew their way around.

We ordered a couple of drinks, and I was looking at him, and I said, "What is going on with your kids?" He just said, "I know. I know. Sometimes they can get a little rowdy."

"Rowdy," I said. "You mean disrespectful and out of control? So, you're not going to say or do anything about their behavior?" And he said, "Like what?" "Like whoop their asses!" Are you kidding me? I wish my damn kids WOULD say anything close to that shit. He then just said, "Well, I know I should probably discipline them, but I feel bad for not being around more."

I was thinking to myself, then why aren't you? You live in the same state and the same city, and you live with your parents. What else are you doing aside from working? I do not feel sorry for you. As a matter of fact, you should be ashamed of yourself. At this point, I really don't have anything else to say about that, except that it was a major turn off for me.

Ok, back to where I was. This was why I wasn't all excited that his kids were going to be joining us. I wasn't sure if I was gonna have to save Anthony from getting jumped by his own kids. Lol. Alright, back to the game.

His friend did get us good seats, and we even got on the Jumbotron. We all had a good time with no incident(s). After the game, we all piled into the van and headed to his cousin's again. Right about now, I wanted to have my own space instead of being in someone's house. I totally assumed that he would have gotten us a hotel room, but I noticed that this guy right here could sleep on the floor if it meant he didn't have to pay for the floor space.

"I'm getting a room. I'm not staying at nobody's house one more night. It's New Year's Eve, and I need my own space to get ready for the night," I told him.

We got into an argument about that. What was there to argue about, you ask? Well, he was trying to convince me that staying in a crowded house was no big deal because they hardly saw him.

"Ok, well, you stay here and let them look at your ass all night. Find me a hotel right now, and I'll pay for it myself, and you can stay here where you belong."

I arrived at a hotel by myself because I refused to let that looser stay with me. Petty or not, I had had it with his cheap ass. No good ass Nigga... yeah, I said it!

It was now later that night, and Anthony had been blowing up my phone since I got there. I texted him to have Tony call me. You remember Tony and Lisa from the Jazz festival? Well, he was with Anthony. My phone rang, and it was Tony.

"I don't have anything to say to your

sorry-ass friend," I told him.

"Oh, come on, we're going to have a good time tonight," he said.

"The only way I'm going tonight is if you pick me up. You and Lisa," I said.

He informed me he was not with Lisa anymore. "Well, whoever your date is tonight, I will ride with you guys," I responded.

He finally gave in and said, "Alright, then that's what we'll do."

I got ready and put on my tight black dress and heels. You know the one, the come fuck me dress. Yeah, that one. A couple of hours later, I got a text saying they were downstairs. I came down and I saw Tony and the new girl Tina. I thanked Tony for picking me up. Then I saw Anthony in the background, looking like a predator in that same beat up black leather jacket. I just rolled my eyes and said, "Ok, I am ready to have a good time now. How about you guys?" They smiled and agreed.

We got to the spot. It was a nice club, pretty good size, so we were not all on top of each other like some clubs can be. I was finally having a good time. It was a good vibe, good crowd, and I was doing some good drinking. I was mingling a little, and a couple

126

of guys started up conversations. Calm down, nothing crazy. I mean, I'm not a total asshole. I knew Anthony's hawk eyes were all over me, so I was not going to disrespect anyone. I wanted to dance. And since Anthony didn't ask me (you know, because he doesn't dance), I accepted another guy's invitation to cut a rug. While I was on the dance floor, I saw Anthony had made his way to Tony, and they were eyeballing me the whole time, which was ok because I noticed quite a few other eyeballs on me as well. I thanked the guy for the dance and made my way back to my drink.

You're probably wondering what I was going to do about Anthony. To tell you the truth, I was all done with this relationship. The guy had no clue how to keep a good woman. And stop it, I know what you're thinking. It was not about money. It wasn't the fact that he didn't have any or even decent credit for that matter. It was about being thoughtful and at least trying to do little things, especially since he was totally broke. It was also about the whole big picture and if I could see a future with him. You're probably wondering why I thought he was broke. I mean, look at all the signs. He got me a Christmas card for Christmas. A "meal"

127

for my birthday and fought with me about getting a hotel room. He didn't have shit, and he wasn't shit! And I was totally done with this shit!

A few days later, I got a long e-mail from you know who. Yup, your boy Anthony, saying how sorry he was for how things turned out. The reason why he didn't get me anything for Christmas or my birthday was that he was BROKE! Let me say that again for the people in the back... he was BROKE!!! Shocker right. I knew it... I fuckin' already knew that shit. He went on to say what an amazing woman and mother I was. How I deserved all the happiness in the world, and he was sorry he wasn't the one who could give it to me, and he would always regret not stepping up. Oh, and he ended with saying that he would always remember me as the one who got away. Say what? The one who got away... more like the one who escaped and ran away. Lol. I mean, that shit was funny. I can actually laugh about it now. I am no longer plotting a murder in the desert. Hey, that could be another book. Lol.

Ok, listen, I have no more interest in Anthony. Zero. That horse has been beaten to a bloody pulp, and it died. No offense to animal lovers because I love animals as well.

But you get the point. The point is that it was not about money and what he did or did not get me. It was that he didn't even think of me at all. All he had to do was communicate with me. He should have told me his situation instead of making up shit and not telling me the truth. Because if he had, we probably would still be together.

The more I look back, it seems that in the whole relationship he did that, not communicate what was really going on with him. All the short cuts, so he wouldn't have to spend any money. Who fuckin' lives like that? That muthafucker, Anthony, that's who. He lived like that. I mean, shit, he lived with his parents. But in my defense, I didn't know that until halfway through this relationship.

The lesson here is what? Don't ignore those muther-lovin' red flags!!! I mean, what did I think was going to happen? He was going to miraculously transform into a thoughtful, responsible, and considerate man who stands on his own two feet and takes care of himself and his business? Damn shame at his age that he didn't want to do that on his own. But come on, you can't make someone grow up if they don't want to. I wanted a mature grownup relationship,

129

and hell, I don't know what he wanted because it sure was not the same thing that I did. I wanted us to always be honest and communicate about everything. But unfortunately, this is what people do. They get together and never have important conversations. They avoid them, and next thing you know, two years go by, and you don't know any more about each other than you did when you first met.

Well, thank the Lord it had only been six months. But in those six months, I did learn a lot about Anthony. I learned that he was at a standstill with his life, didn't like responsibility, and wasn't trying to change or better himself or his life at all. That is the reason why I am not with him. Looking back, I do feel that I dodged a major bullet. Thank you, Jesus! Because I know eventually his kids would have killed him and tried to cover it up thinking their dumb asses could get away with it. So, for that, I am very thankful.

After Anthony, I needed to take a break from dating for a minute. I was so exhausted. But even after a bad ending, I never gave up on love — never have, never will. Every man is not the same. But now I am taking a long look at myself and asking, "Why do I keep getting the same result?" They are not the same situations or the same men, but they are the same results. It can't be everyone else all of the time. Can it?

CHAPTER SIX: DECEPTION

My online experiences so far have ranged from entertaining, exhausting, and a lot of just no matches. But I have never been catfished or just flat out deceived until now. So here is my one and only experience with that.

DECEPTION

Alright, here we go. I decided to try the dating site Plenty of Fish, aka POF. I heard about it — good things and not-so-good things. I figured what the hell, I'd see for myself. I created a profile and spun the wheel. I started getting a bunch of messages that ranged from 'Hi, can we meet? Would love to take you out,' to 'You are the woman of my dreams, Will you marry me,' and my favorite, 'Why are you even on here?' Over time, I very quickly started feeling like a little fish swimming among sharks. Very hungry sharks. I started sifting through messages and pictures. I responded here and there, mostly just thank yous. Mainly trying to be polite, but I quickly realized that that wasn't a good idea. Because if I was not interested, it seemed any communication was a lifeline, even if they were lying on their death bed, in a coma, and on life support, any response gave them hope.

I went out a few times here and there. Nothing crazy, just dates that didn't work out. At times, I started chit-chatting with a guy, and if our conversations were going well, I started thinking they looked better than they really did. But when we met, it quickly brought me right back to reality and then, "It's a no for me, dawg." Damn that Randy Jackson!

I started chatting with a guy, "John." I saw his pictures, and he was cute. He had different pics with friends and family, and they were full-body pics, not just face pics. Except one, it was a terrible selfie. His eyes were kinda bulging, but I think he took it way too close. I don't know why guys don't care and post any ole thing…SMH.

After having conversations on the POF site, he gave me his number, so we could talk. One night, I called him, and we had a good conversation. We exchanged our different upbringing and backgrounds, and it went well. He asked me why I was on here, and I told him, "Just like everyone else, I'm dating, trying to find a companion." He agreed with that, and we talked about meeting. I noticed he kept saying he was in no rush. He wanted to get to know me, so talking on the phone was good. He wanted me to be very comfortable before we met. My response to that was as it always was, I would rather meet sooner than later so nobody wasted anybody's time. I explained the longer we continued messaging and talking on the phone, the more attached we would get, and if and when we met, if one of us wasn't feeling the other, that would suck for the other person. I was trying to avoid any awkwardness, so that didn't happen, and I didn't want to feel bad if I didn't have any attraction after we met. His response to that was, "Yeah, that does make sense, and I really do want to meet you, but I don't want to mess things up."

The next day, I went to work, and we texted throughout the day. I got off a little early, so I figured I'd call John and see what he was up to that night so we could maybe meet up for a drink. I called him while I was driving home. He was very happy to hear from me, so I asked him if he wanted to meet up for a drink. He started getting kind of worked up.

"Oh, wow, really, now? Ok, ok, you really want to meet up?" he began.

"Yeah, don't you?" I asked.

"Yes, I really want to see you. You seem like a really cool girl, and you are so beautiful," he answered and kept rambling on. "Ok, ok this is crazy. I'm not right, I'm not right."

"Ok, look, you either want to meet up, or you don't. It doesn't have to be right now. It can be a little later so you can get ready or finish whatever you're doing and get right," I reassure him.

"Ok, ok, that sounds good. So, what time and where?" he asked.

"How about 7 o'clock? He wanted to make it 7:30. "Ok, that's fine."

I asked him what area he was in so we could figure out a spot. Shockingly enough, I knew the area, so I suggested Claim Jumper, which was not too far from the both of us. He knew where it was and agreed to meet at that time and place. We hung up. I got home, freshened up, and headed out about 7:10.

Ok, here we go. I pulled up, and I was in a good mood, hoping at the very least we continued with our good conversation that we'd been having for the past week. I walked in, and it was pretty empty. I walked up to where the hostess was supposed to be, but she was not there. I started looking around, and then I saw two people who saw me, and I noticed them whisper to each other and acted like that must be her. One of them came over to me and said, "Are you waiting for someone? I said, "Yes."

I have to say, I was getting this weird vibe. It was like everyone was looking at me and seemed to know why I was there. Very strange. Never experienced this before. I have to say, I never saw what was coming. Nope, not in a million years.

Ok, she was walking me to the bar side of the restaurant where there were booths, and I saw John, or who I thought was John, standing next to the booth. As I got closer, it looked like he was holding onto the side of the booth to help him stand. The closer I got, I saw that his appearance was much different than his pictures. Ok, well, remember when I said one of his pictures was really close up, so it kind of made his eyes look really big kind of bulging? Well, it wasn't a bad picture, it was the only one that came close to how he really looked.

I was standing in front of him, and I

smiled and said, "Hi, it's good to see you," and gave him a quick hug. I did that so it wouldn't seem like we'd just met because it seemed like everyone was looking at us. He tried to sit down, but I could see it was a struggle to do that. He finally sat down and looked at me and said, "This isn't what you expected, huh?" I just looked at him with raised eyebrows, but I didn't say anything. He started talking and trying to explain himself. He apologized for not being upfront with me and said he was scared that I wouldn't have wanted to meet him or even talk to him if I knew he had MS. I don't know anything about MS, but I was pretty sure he wasn't in the beginning stages because of his appearance and the fact that he could barely stand on his own. Like I said, his eyes were kind of bulging, and his face had a certain look to it. He couldn't stand on his own for very long, and he needed a walker to walk. That explained why he got there so early.

John figured he should tell me the whole story.

He said that about 4 years back, he was at a club with his girlfriend at the time and some friends. I guess he used to be very much into the street life. Another thing I didn't know. He suddenly started to get this pain in his legs, he fell to the floor, and he couldn't move. He didn't know what was happening to him. They had to call an ambulance, and it got worse for him from there. Shortly thereafter, he was diagnosed with MS and that he was going to get progressively worse as time went on. And he did.

He slowly started to feel more pain and lose mobility, and his appearance started to change as well. He had to change his diet, and he started really smoking weed to help with the pain. And as this started to happen, he went into a depression and pushed his then-girlfriend away because he was having a hard time dealing with/accepting what was happening to him. He said he lived with his dad, and he took care of him. He said he finally recently started coping with the disease and had started trying to get out of the house.

Ok, I know you're probably wondering what was going on in my mind right this second, right? Ok, fair question. I was in total shock, blown away, and all I could do was smile and nod to keep from crying. I know what you're thinking—why the hell weren't you angry and pissed at the fact that he lied to you and wasn't upfront about having MS??? And why didn't you head for the exit, like 20 minutes ago? I don't know why. But maybe because I'm a human being, and so was he. All I can say is that I was totally caught off guard. I didn't see this coming at all. I felt frozen. Never in my wildest dreams would I have thought anything like this would happen to me. At the same time, I felt nothing but compassion deceived me, no question about that. But hearing him talk and how he totally opened up to me, I knew he hadn't had very many conversations like that before. I felt so bad for him and to think that it could happen to anyone. I mean, he had no clue at all, and bam, his life was changed forever. He continued telling me that most of his friends stopped coming around, so he had no one to talk to. At that point, I tried to look and sound normal, so I tried to keep my questions to a minimum so he wouldn't feel uncomfortable. Ok, more uncomfortable.

I ended up ordering food and drinks. I was trying to give him a little bit of normalcy, even if it was just for a couple of hours. But the more he talked about his depression, the more I found it hard to keep that smile. At one point, he said, "You're not gonna cry, are you?" All I could say was, "I'm sorry. I'm fine." Then he said, "I'm ok. I just really want to thank you for coming and staying and having dinner with me." I smiled and told him I was enjoying myself.

I excused myself and went to the bathroom. While I was in the bathroom, I told myself, "keep it together, you're almost done. There is nothing you can do for him so stop thinking there." I got back to the table and asked if he was ready to go.

"You can go ahead and go," he said. "No, we can walk out together," I said.

"I have to call my dad to pick me up. He dropped me off. So, you can go ahead and go."

"Well, I can drop you off. Where do you live?" He told me, and I said, "Ok, that's on my way. He asked me if I was sure. I kept trying to reassure him that it was not a problem, so he finally agreed. He called over the waitress and asked for her to bring over his walker. The waitress looked confused and asked the other waitress, and she said, "Yes, we have it over here."

We made it outside, and it was January, so it was freezing. Yes, people, it gets cold in Arizona. I started walking, then he stopped and asked me where my car was? I pointed to the black Range Rover Evoque. I saw him pause, so I asked him if I should bring it around? He said, yeah, that it would take him a while to walk over there. I went and got the car and brought it around to where he was. I opened the back door so he could put his walker in the backseat because I knew it wouldn't fit in the small trunk, but we were having trouble getting it in there too. I mean, we were really having trouble getting it inside the car. We were trying different angles, but it wouldn't fit. OMG!! We burst into laughter. We were really looking like fools out here, trying to get this damn walker in the car. Finally, we got it in. Well, I got it in, and we both jumped in the car before we froze to death. He was doing all the talking as I drove. Basically, he was trying to convince me to be his friend. He told me that he smoked weed because it helped with his pain and nerves, and for some reason, I got the feeling that might not be all he did as far as drugs.

We finally got to his place. I got his walker out of the back seat and helped him to the door. I gave him a hug and thanked him for dinner, and I walked away before he had a chance to say anything else. As I was driving off, I could no longer hold it in. I started to cry uncontrollably. That was the saddest thing ever. My heart broke for him. I felt his sadness and desperation, and it was the saddest thing. I really thought about being his friend because I felt he really needed one. But I also thought about the reality of the situation, which was he lived in a bad area, and who knew who else hung around him and what he did as far as drugs. Everything did not seem on the up and up. For those reasons and the fact that he wasn't even honest about his situation from the beginning, I didn't think it was a good idea. Mainly for safety reasons, but that still made me feel like total shit. But I was dating, not trying to be a social worker. See, trying to get thicker skin but damn, this was a rough one.

CHAPTER SEVEN: EXHAUSTED

Alright, here is where my head was at this point. I'd been online dating off and on for a little while. I'd been on dates, and it was getting frustrating not to have found a lasting match. To put it frankly, I was fuckin' tired and getting worn down. So, this is where men start looking better to you that didn't before, and you agree to date them. I know it's kind of fucked up, but it is what it is. This is what happens when you do that.

Tony was tall and looked like he was in reasonable shape. He had pictures posted of his home, his nice car, and I think that was a Jacuzzi. Yup, it was a Jacuzzi. Hmmm... Why hmmm, you ask? Well, because sometimes. when certain pictures are posted, they are trying to give you subliminal hints. Just saying. Ok, so here we go.

Tony sent me a message and was very chatty and definitely very social. He was very complimentary — tons of compliments. You know the type. You are too fine. Damn, you're fine. How is your fine ass out here alone in these streets?

He seemed to have a very cool personality. Good phone conversation, no awkward silence, and he was forward, which I liked. He wasted no time in getting a date set up, which was great, so we didn't waste anyone's time. We met up at a little bar/pizza shop to do a meet and greet. I believe that's what he called it. He told me that he had also been on dates that didn't amount to anything, so basically, he didn't want to keep spending money on dinner. He thought I didn't know what was up. But it was cool. I had no problem with that at all because it was only for a drink, and then no harm, no foul.

I pulled up and walked up to the door. It was pretty empty, so kind of hard to miss him. I was trying to remember what his pictures looked like in my head so I could compare them to the live person. Too late, he waved me down. He was pretty much the only Black dude there, so I knew it was him. SMH. Damn! He was a #3. Oh well.

He was older than I was by about 7 years. He was very talkative and the life-of-the-party type. Just tons of personality, which was good because he didn't even notice my disinterest in him. Or maybe he did and was ignoring it. I think it was all about trying to make it work in his eyes. We talked about the usual background stuff, where you're from, why you're still single, and what you are looking for. Ok, I have to say, he was definitely not my type. I mean, his hair was a little thin at the top, probably a year away from needing Bosley or just go all the way bald. Make a choice. He was not in the best of shape. He told me he had surgery on one of his knees, so he walked with a slight limp. I will say, he really did have the gift of gab, though. Because he had a great personality, you know the kind where you think you have your mind made up, then next thing you know, you've just been talked into going out again but this time to a Suns game. I was driving home, and that's exactly what happened. I was like what the heck just happened? I'm going to the Suns game tomorrow? SMH.

He kept texting me throughout the day to make sure I didn't change my mind. You know the "Good morning beautiful" texts and more random texts. He was pretty smart because he figured if he kept talking and kept me laughing, I wouldn't change my mind. But I wouldn't. I told you I'm not like that. Once I make a commitment, I keep it.

Maybe I should change that about myself.

I was going to meet him straight from work at a grocery store parking lot, so we could figure out where to park my car. We decided to just leave it there in the Safeway parking lot until after the game. I got there first and waited in my car for about 5 minutes. Then he pulled up in his S-Class Mercedes Benz, loud music playing, and he had someone in the car with him. He saw me and said, "Come here, girl. Don't be shy!" I looked at him, and then I looked at his friend. He said, "Oh, this is," whatever his name was, "I was just giving him a ride."

I thought to myself, a ride to where? We were at a grocery store. Damn just Nigga shit!

"You ready, because I am?" he said.

Alright, let's do this. As we drove to the game, he had the music up real loud. Ok, normally, I wouldn't mind because I have some hood in me too, so I like that shit too. However, that only really works when you are with someone you actually like. Because otherwise, you are attracting a lot of attention, and it can be rather embarrassing. You know what I mean. That's why I could never have a sugar daddy because I could never handle the stares and the whispering.

And I would never want to one day blurt out, "Ok, stop! I can't do this shit no more!" Lol. Sorry I digress. Back to Tony.

We were driving to the arena, and he was having a ball, bobbing his head to the music J Cole "Work Out." And damn, that song started to get me going to... Hey... "Straight up now tell me do you really wanna luv me forever... Oh Oh Oh"... Ok, damn, let me stop. You get the picture. Sometimes when you start feeling good, you start thinking, well, maybe he's not that bad. Well, that's where I was. Oh, did I mention he worked for the Suns in some capacity—not sure exactly what. That's why he was taking me to the game, aside from the fact that he clearly wanted to impress me because I told him I loved basketball.

We pulled up to the arena. People seemed to know him. We drove in, and I guess he had a designated spot. Ok, ok, you've got my attention, Sir.

Everyone seemed to know Tony, and apparently, Tony was now the man. You know what I mean. He was introducing me to everyone, and they looked at me and then him, and were like, ok, Tony, and they nodded their heads. But you know what, I was ok with that because at that moment we were having a good time, and I was being treated like he was really appreciating that I had come with him. So what if it was never going to go any further than that night. He had a smile on his face, and he was happy, so I was good with that.

He walked me down the tunnel and then to the area where there was a buffet of food. I forgot what that area is called. We ate a little, got a drink, and headed to our seats. Now, keep in mind I hate bad seats remember. I mean, if it's not seven rows or less, I'm not going. I'd rather watch at home. Just saying that's just me. I believe I mentioned that to him before we came. Well, guess who had seats right behind the sports casters' table? Yup, us. Lol. I believe those were floor seats. I'm sure he was able to pull some strings to get these seats, but I really didn't care, I was enjoying the ride. Just as long as the ride kept his hands to himself. You know what I'm saying.

I don't remember who the Suns were playing, but it was a good game. It is now half-time, and they were doing the kiss cam. I know you can guess what was happening here. He started paying close attention to the Jumbotron or whatever it's called. Son of a Bitch! Don't fuckin' do it! That's all I kept

148

thinking in my head. But then I was thinking, come on, you know this muthafucker is going to do it. And sure enough, I see us on the big screen, and everyone's eyes are on us, yelling kiss, kiss, and nudging both of us. Mainly me because they saw the look I had on my face. Shit, there was no way I could get out of it. Why is it taking so long to move on? So, I did what any reasonable person would do when you are caught on the kiss cam, and thousands of eyes are on you. I turned my head the other way, and half smiled so it would go away. And there, finally, it's over, right? Nope, here it comes again. Son of a bleep!!! I believe he set it all up, but it wasn't going away. I just looked at him, and he went in to kiss me. I slightly turned my head, and he landed on my cheek. I put my hands on his cheeks, so it didn't look that bad for him. I heard clapping, and finally, it was over. I can tell he was disappointed. But oh fuckin' well! Nobody told you to do that, especially when you're not getting any 'I want to kiss you' vibes from me. So, I don't feel sorry for you at all. But I couldn't blame him for trying.

We finished watching the game, but I could tell he knew what the inevitable was. On the ride back to my car, he was not as talkative as before. It was like dead man walking. Whelp, I gave him a hug, and I thanked him for the game, and he said no problem. I know he knew that was the last time we would ever see each other.

I got home, and later I got this text from him. At first, he was saying he hoped I had a good time. I replied, "Yes, I did." Then I was thinking I was going to have to cut the cord on this one because the guy was not getting the hint at all. I got the feeling he might get a little aggressive/pushy at some point and wouldn't take rejection all that well. So, I told him, "I think you are a really nice guy, but I don't think we are a match. I hope you find what you are looking for, take care." I figured instead of avoiding calls and texts, I would tell him, and he would appreciate my honesty, and there should be nothing left to say about it. Right? Wrong. Well, he responded alright. He proceeded to cuss me out. Saying, "You ain't shit!" I've been with finer women than you." Yikes, he was pretty angry. Of course, I had to get my 2 cents in there too. Peg-leg muthafucker! But after that, I blocked him because this was pointless.

Do I feel bad, you ask? Not even a little for letting him take you out? No, I do not.

Because when we met, I told him I wouldn't mind being his friend. He knew I wasn't into him or his fucked-up leg. But he kept talking and talking until I finally agreed to go out with him again. So, there you have it. Another unsuccessful match. But I have to admit, this was a fun one. Lol.

As more time went by, I learned to enjoy the ride. It is all about the journey, no matter how much of a shitty result you end up getting.

Remember when I said, "the Good, the Bad, and the Ugly". Well, this next one was definitely one of the UGLY ones. With that being said, let's get started on the next ride.

CHAPTER EIGHT: VIRGINA BEACH

I began sifting through messages and pictures that went with those pictures. Ok, here's one. He was a good-looking guy — good pictures — like four of them. Ok, ok, I thought we might have something here. His messages to me were compliments, which was always a good thing, especially when you also liked his pics. So far, so good.

We started chit-chatting then we exchanged numbers. We texted then had phone conversations. I have to admit, I was feeling pretty good about this one. He was in the military, which I was ok with. That meant security, right? Come on, girls, I know that's what you think of when you meet a military man. Aside from the military, he was also going to school for something in legal field. Ok, cool.

I told him about myself, and he was delighted, to say the least. We were having good conversations as the days went by. We were talking non-stop and texting in between our calls. You know the regular shit that happens when you like someone. It had not been quite three weeks since we'd met online. Just as we were about to set something up to get together, he told me he was being deployed to Iraq. Say what! Come again.

I know you're thinking, uh, he's in the military, of course, you must know that is always a possibility. And you are right, but that really was the furthest thing from my mind. Well, now it is a reality. Shit, what was a girl to do now? Well, duh. I was going to keep talking to him, of course. Lol. I know some of you would have probably gotten off the train here since it is way too early to know if it would workout. But I am the opposite. I will ride shit out till the wheels fall off. And that's exactly what I did. This is definitely a flaw I need to work on. But my motto has always been, you'll never know if you don't try. I really gotta change my motto.

Once Lee left for Iraq, our communication became very limited. When I say limited, I mean, I had to wait for him to call me in order for us to talk because he didn't have access to a phone on a regular basis. We went from talking at least once a day and constantly texting, to talking maybe once or twice a week. It was hard especially when I got so used to talking to him. Oh, and get this, he would be in Iraq for SIX MONTHS!!! Yes, you read that right.

Again, I know this is where a lot of you would jump ship. But nope, not me. Trying to enjoy that fuckin' ride, remember? A couple of things were going through my mind with the decision to continue with Lee. 1) It was a good chance to get to know each other because we had no choice but to communicate about every and anything. 2) Instead of going off looks and physical attraction, I was forced to get to know him and not jump into bed (oh shit, did I just give myself away? and 3) Nothing had worked so far, and I'd never done 1 and 2 so what the hell, let me give it a try and just maybe it would all work out.

As the days and weeks went by, believe it or not, things were going really well. At least they were going well until I decided to go to my boss's dinner party. Lee called me while I was there. I didn't hear my phone. At least not the first time he called. I saw the missed call, but it wasn't like I could call him back. Iraq, remember. A little while later, my phone rang, and it was Lee again. I had hoped he would call back. I answered the phone with a smile on my face.

"Hey, I'm so glad you called back." I didn't get a warm reception.

"Where were you when I called you the first time? And why didn't you answer?"

Well, damn. Before I could explain that I was not at home, I was at my boss's little party, Lee started with, "Don't you know how hard it is to be able to call you? I told you before, I don't get access to a phone on a regular basis, so I have to call when I can."

My boss saw me and walked up to me because he saw a look of bewilderment on my face. All I could say was, "Yes, I understand. Ok...right."

After he was done scolding me like an 8-year- old, he said, "I really miss you and can't wait for us to be together."

I walked into the bathroom to get some privacy and said, "I miss you too." I really didn't think anything of it. I just took it as he was getting frustrated being so far away as was I.

One day while I was at work, he called. I answered, and we were having a good conversation, except this time it turned into something a little odd. We'd had a couple of previous conversations that we had a difference of opinion about. The particulars are really not important. What is important is that he was turning this conversation into a lesson. The last time we'd spoken, he'd said he wanted me to think about our conversation, "and the next time we talk, I want you to tell me what you've learned." At that moment, I just said, "Ok, sure. I'll do that." But I honestly did not think he was serious. I guess I was wrong because apparently, he was "dead ass serious." Since I didn't answer him, he asked me again, "So what did you learn?" I know what you're thinking. Is this guy for real? Because I was thinking the same thing at that moment. Well, yup, he was. I decided to entertain the bullshit and gave him a bullshit response so we could be done and move on. After going back and forth longer than I should have since I was at work, we were finally done, and we finally moved on.

I was not really sure what was happening other than maybe he was a little bit of a control freak. He seemed to want to control every situation, no matter how insignificant it was. Ok, you're probably saying maybe that was a red flag you should have been paying attention to. I don't know, maybe, but right now, I didn't think so. You know how it goes. You are so into someone that you don't notice anything bad about the person. Why do we do this? I guess that was me. Ignoring anything bad.

Believe it or not, that wasn't the last time we had those strange conversations. I know, surprise, surprise, right? However, I was not deterred at all. We'd had plenty of great conversations that had left me wanting more. And when I say more, I mean wanting some dick. Sorry, just trying to make you understand how I was feeling at the time.

Oh, and Lee apparently thought I needed to see his because, during one of our conversations, we talked about me needing pictures of him (regular ole recent pictures.) BTW, I had previously sent him pictures of myself. You know me, I always want to make sure we always know what we look like! I cannot stress that enough, people. So, there are, say it with me, NO SUPRISES!!! Well, I guess he wanted to make sure I knew what his penis looked like because, yup, you guessed it, he sent me a dick pic. SMDH. I am definitely not that nasty type. And yes, if you like dick pics, you are Nasty! I am more of an undercover nasty. I really did not appreciate the dick pic at all. The reason I was so surprised was because we definitely didn't talk about sending each other nasty pictures. If I had thought this was on his mind, I would have told him, "Do not send me no shit like that, nasty." Not into that at all. You can imagine my face when I opened his e-mail and Boom! A Dick! So tacky. Oh, and get this, the message part in the e-mail read, "Enjoy!" Wow. I just asked you for pictures. Just recent fuckin' pictures.

Alright, I know what you're wondering. Was it big or little? You nasty muthafuckers! But I guess if I had to judge, it was a pretty good size! Lol. But seriously, the next time I spoke with him, I did tell him I really needed some recent pictures. Especially since he never sent me any. He always seemed to have an excuse why he didn't. Then he left for Iraq, so I just left it alone. Oh yeah, he did send me some pictures while he was there, but they were the same ones that were on the site.

I know what you're thinking, this was a definite red flag. Maybe. But he did say he was going to send me some after his little ceremony. He was getting some award there for something. I can't even remember for what. I know I'm a shitty girlfriend, but damn, I am sexually deprived, and that's all

158

I could think about. I mean, shit, I already knew I was going straight to Hell. After I reminded him again where were my pictures, I finally got an e-mail. Finally! I opened the e-mail, and there were about 5 pictures; a couple of him in regular clothes and a few in his uniform and then one taken of him receiving an award for whatever it was for. Damn. Looking at the pictures, I guess he was in between a #2 and #3. I mean, I knew it was him, and they weren't terrible, but let's just say I wasn't jumping for joy. In fact, if it weren't for all the time I put in with this guy, I would have walked away.

Ok, now let's assess this WHOLE situation. I was a little disappointed after seeing his pictures. But I felt like I really knew him, and we had a really good thing going. So, he wasn't perfect, and he was definitely no Boris Kodjoe or Blair Underwood. But so what. So, that was where I was at, and I was moving forward.

After many, many conversations, some scoldings, unwanted dick pics, and some disappointing pictures, I thought we were in a good place and had gotten to know each other pretty well. Everything had not been perfect, but nothing ever is. The months had rolled on by, and it had been six whole months that we'd been doing this song and dance, and yes, we were in an actual relationship. I mean, hell, we'd been planning our pretend wedding for months. Lol. You know you've done it too, so don't act like I'm the only one.

It was December, and he was due to return to American soil. Here was the plan, I was going to take a week off from work, and he was going to fly to Arizona to me first, then go home to Virginia Beach. I was really excited to finally be able to see, touch, and do whatever we felt like doing to each other. You know what I'm saying.

It was a Thursday, my last day at work. Lee was flying into another state, laying over there for the night instead of doing a straight billion hours back. He said he would call me when he got in that night. But I didn't hear from him until early the next morning. When I did talk to him, he was not in the mood I thought he would be in. He sounded kind of grouchy and irritated that I'd been worried/concerned about him. I mean, he even snapped at me and said, "I was traveling all day and night, so when I got to the hotel, I just crashed out." But he said it like I had no reason to be concerned at all, even though my reason to be concerned was

160

that his plane could have crashed into the muthafuckin' ocean muthafucker! But ok, ok, just let it go. Let's not start this on the wrong foot. Right.

He told me he was getting ready to leave for the airport to catch his flight to me. His tone had changed, hopefully, because he realized how shitty he sounded. Either way, it really didn't matter because the reality was that the day had come when in a few short hours, we would finally meet face to face.

Was I nervous, you ask? Hell yes! Because now, I was thinking about all the things that could go wrong. I know, I know... you're thinking, Bitch, you're just now thinking about this shit? Well, it's not that I never thought about it, it's just that I felt like there was more good than bad when I did. But at this moment, I wasn't so sure anymore. It seemed like it was one thing after another. But you know what, my motto hasn't changed. "You'll never know if you don't try." And I'm sticking to that, even if it kills me. Literally.

In our last conversation, he wanted me to wear a dress to the airport. I said ok, even though it was the middle of winter, and again, even if people think it doesn't get cold in Arizona, it really does. It's the damn desert, people. It was going to be like low 50s when I picked him up. But ok, fuck it... here I go.

I arrived at the airport at about 11:00 p.m. and in time to park and get to arrivals. Oh, what was I wearing? A long sleeve fitted black dress just below the knee with a black leather jacket and brown boots that had a 3 inch heel. Walking through the airport, it was pretty empty, but I was getting looks and stares while I was getting to the correct gate. I was thinking because who goes to the airport wearing club attire? But that was what he wanted, and I was there to please my man.

I was waiting along with a few others who were also waiting for their loved ones or friends. After a little while, it seemed that everyone had left except me. Then I saw Lee coming down the escalator. At least I thought it was him because this man I saw coming down was wearing glasses! And not sunglasses like Usher because no one should do that except Usher. I mean regular glasses. The reason it was a big deal was that I had never seen him in glasses. He had never mentioned that he wore glasses. And there was no sign of glasses in any of his pictures. So, was that really a big deal, you ask? Hell yes, it was! Because glasses alter your appearance. It wasn't like eyelashes or fake

nails. And in some cases, glasses make you look like a totally different person. And this was one of these muthafuckin' cases. They were kind of thick and made his eyes look beady. You know what I'm talking about—that pervert look. Damn.

As he was coming down, I had this look of disappointment, but I quickly put on a smile and got it together. We hugged, and I think he saw that look I had on my face because his demeanor changed to like oh, you're not a big deal. I asked him how his flight was, and he said it was ok, but he was so glad to be in Arizona. As we were walking, all you heard was the heels of my boots clicking. He said, "You look nice, but those boots killed it." Not sure what he meant by that, but I'll have you know, I've always gotten compliments on these boots.

"I didn't know you wore glasses. You never mentioned that important bit of information," I said to him.

"Yes, I did," he responded.

I was thinking, then Maury needs to strap your ass to that lie detector because that is a WHOLE LIE! We got to my car, and I felt like, WTF did I get myself into? But it was seriously too late to back out. We drove to my place, and he kept saying, "I am so glad to finally be here." As for me, I didn't know really how I felt right now. I felt like I was deceived, and I was trying to get over it and make the best of it. I mean, even without his glasses, I just wasn't impressed.

We got to my house, and it was late like almost midnight I assumed he'd already eaten, so one less thing to worry about. We went upstairs to my room, and I showed him where he could put his things. I told him I was really tired, and I went straight to bed, and so did he, so don't even think about anything else happening.

The next morning, I heard him up and rambling through his bags. I got up and walked into the bathroom and saw that he had put out ALL his toiletries. Ok, let me explain. A normal person, I would expect, would have a toothbrush, toothpaste, and mouth wash. You get it, the usual stuff, right. Well, what I saw was toothbrushes, toothpastes, mouth washes, deodorants, shaving creams, razors, soaps, lotions, face soaps. PLURAL. And everything was sprawled out on the counter as if it was his bathroom. First of all, why would you need to unpack everything you brought? You are only going to be here one week. Second of all, why is there more than two of everything like you buy in bulk? And again, why did you unpack everything??? It seemed a little weird. It looks like you are about to have a yard sale here in my bathroom. But, ok, whatever.

We went downstairs to figure out what we wanted to get into that day. I turned the t.v. on and sat on the couch, and he was sitting across from me, and we started small-talking. As I was looking at him, I had to admit I was not really feeling that attracted to him, but I kept thinking about all our conversations and all the time I'd already spent with him via the telephone. I decided I was going to really give it the good ole college try.

I felt like he was reading my mind because next thing I knew, he came to sit next to me, and he kissed me. Ok, yes, maybe it would be better if I closed my eyes and just let go. So, I did. Then he started to move lower and lower and lower until he arrived at the final destination. I had to admit, it was feeling good. Ok, really fuckin' good! But then he abruptly stopped. He sat up and looked at me and said, "I don't think you're ready for this yet." It was like the record player scratches off the record. You know the sound I'm talking about. But maybe it was a good thing because it snapped me back into reality. And the reality was that he looked like a pervert with those damn glasses. You know the creepy man who owned one of those 70's vans that drove slow during school hours. That kind. So, back to the moment.

"You know, you are probably right." I pulled my shorts up and said, "So, what do you want to do today? I was thinking we could go to breakfast and then we can go from there."

"You didn't go grocery shopping before I came?" "Well, no, because I didn't know what you do or don't like. I figured we could go together." He had this real irritated look on his face like that was a dumb idea. I just looked at him and said, "I didn't want to get things you didn't eat or are allergic to." He rolled his eyes. Then I got up and went upstairs. I was going to get in the shower and get dressed because I didn't know what in the holy hell was happening right now.

Ok, so pay attention. Remember when I said I have experienced the Good the Bad, and the Ugly? Well, this was starting to get to the UGLY part. I was in the shower with the door locked, and I was thinking, how could I get out of this because it was getting weirder and weirder by the minute. The only thing I came up with was, let's just see how things go. Hopefully, things will get better. Because I don't think you're going to get this muthafucker out of your house. I mean, shit, this bathroom looks like he's already moved in.

I got dressed, and I heard Lee coming up the stairs. He was on the phone, talking to someone. From what I heard, he was talking about his grandmother being sick and in the hospital. Once he hung up, he told me that his grandmother had been in the hospital for a couple of days and was not doing well. I told him I was sorry to hear that. Then I asked him what he wanted to do today. He looked at me with this crazy look and said, "Did you not just hear what I said? I said my grandmother is in the hospital and not doing well."

"Ok, so do you need to leave to go be with her?" I asked.

He looked down and said, "No, I'm going to wait and see if she gets better."

I was really feeling like this whole thing was a terrible mistake, especially me thinking that by talking for six months, we would actually know each other. Because right at this moment, I could honestly say, "I DON'T KNOW THIS MUTHAFUCKER AT ALL!!!" It seemed like everything I said he took wrong. The vibe was really fucked up. That was so not what I wanted or thought it would be. However, this is what it was, and there really was no time to be sad or think about anything because this was happening right fuckin' now.

I went into my survival mode. Let's be real here. I had a strange man in my house that I invited for whatever reason. But he was an invited guest. He hadn't threatened me or even showed any aggression toward me, so I didn't want to jump the gun just yet. But make no mistake, I was totally aware of my situation and how it could take a wrong turn at any moment. Ok, that being said, let's get back to it, shall we.

We did absolutely nothing all day. He was on his phone non-stop, and I watched a couple of movies. Definitely not what I had in mind as a vacation. It was now evening time, and I was famished. I went downstairs and said, "You wanna go to the grocery store and get food?"

"Absolutely. That sounds like a great idea." Ok, I didn't know how to feel about his ever-changing mood swings, Sybil. But I was too weak to say anything about it, so off we went grocery shopping. This was what I had in mind, minus the sarcasm I got when I'd brought it up earlier. I need you to know now, after spending a night and a full day with him, I no longer believed we were a match at all. This person who was in my presence was nothing like the person I had been communicating with for six long months. It was a WHOLE lie. This man was an asshole with ever-changing moods and personalities, which was really fucked up because I had not changed at all. I was the same and was acting the same as when we'd first started talking. I take it back, what was changing was my lack of patience. I really was this close to snapping. But I was trying to keep it together long enough to get him on his way without incident.

We made it to Albertson's grocery store. For those of you who are not familiar with this store, it is not cheap like a Food 4 Less or Walmart. Just want you to understand that. In a minute, you will see why. We were in the produce section, and I was pushing the basket. He was looking at apples, oranges, etc., asking if I wanted any of them.

"I don't really want any fruit."

We headed to the first aisle of whatever. He started asking me if I liked this or if I liked that. Sometimes, I said, "Yes, I do like that," and sometimes I said, "I don't." The times I said I do like that, he put the item in the basket. We started going down the next aisle, and he kept asking me the same thing. Do you like this, or do you like that? Sometimes I said yes, and sometimes I said no. We went down the next aisle, and it was the same thing. You get the picture. I noticed a pattern, and the basket was getting filled with things I didn't necessarily want to get. When he started asking again about an item, I stopped him and

I said, "Yes, I like it, but no, I don't want it." I grabbed it from him and put it back. Oh, and BTW, my attitude right now is of extreme irritation and starvation. I was so fuckin hungry that if I had a knife in my hand, I would have used it to gut his ass and eat his liver! That was how hungry I was. And this mutherfucker was acting like one of his Sybil personalities because he looked like he was in the best mood, chit-chatting with people, acting like we'd been having the best time. If he started whistling and skipping and shit, I was leaving.

We were literally going down every single

aisle, and he was putting everything he liked in the basket. For example, we were in the bacon aisle. He was looking at the different kinds of bacon, picked one, put it in the basket, then asked, "You like sausage?" He looked at different brands. Picked up some expensive brand and put it in the basket. I said again, "Ok, that's enough. We don't need 3 different sausages and 3 different bacons!" He shrugged and said, "Ok," and kept walking onto the next aisle.

Ok, what the Fuck was going on? Because I felt like I was being punked. Seriously, that was how I was feeling. I felt like he was making a joke out of it. We were finally getting to the last of the aisles because we had literally gone down every aisle in the whole damn store, and our basket was FULL! I finally said, "Ok, that's enough. We don't need anything else!" He stopped, looked at the basket, and smiled and said, "Yeah, I think we have enough here."

We finally headed to the check out. While we were waiting in line, I told him we were going to have to stop and pick something up because I was starving and too tired to cook anything. There was a Chinese restaurant down the street we could go and grab take-out. He said, "Ok, yes, that sounds good because I know you are starving." I looked at him with a very irritated look on my face, like no shit, Sherlock. Again, he was acting like he was in the best mood. Not sure why or how he got there, and frankly, I didn't give a shit.

He put all the food up on the counter, and I looked at the checkout girl, and I said, "It's a lot of food, huh?" She looked at me and smiled. I felt like she didn't really know what to say because she saw the irritation all over my face, and she saw Lee over there acting like we only had a couple of things. As she was scanning the food, he asked her where the liquor was. She told him she needed to get a key for the cabinet if he wanted any liquor. He looked at me, and I gave him this death stare, so he said, "No, that's ok."

Then he moved in front of me or by the guy bagging the food, not beside me where he should have been. You see where I'm going with this. She rang up the last item, and it read 356 fuckin' dollars! I knew it was going to be some crazy amount. I reached for my purse because normally, when a woman reaches for her purse, the man will stop her and then pull out his wallet. Right? Ok, so he came over to me and said, "Hold on." He reached into his back pocket and pulled out his wallet. While he was doing this, the checker girl and I made eye contact, and she was looking at me like, please let this man pay for all this food, because I think this lady is going to literally physically hurt him if he doesn't.

Well, that's not exactly what happened. He went in his wallet all right, but he only pulled out $60! You read that right, the groceries cost $356, and this man pulled out 60 fuckin' dollars! My initial reaction was to say fuck you and walk out and leave him and his groceries because you know those were his fuckin' groceries, not mine. But me being me, I don't like, and will always avoid, any kind of public embarrassment, so I gave her my card and paid for the basket full of groceries that were enough for more than a damn week and enough for a small African village. I didn't even buy most of that shit for myself when I did go shopping. WTF happened? What kind of man does that? A Bitch Ass Nigga that's what kind! Ok, let me stop because I really needed to calm down. What I was feeling was RAGE. Pure and simple. One step away from seeing red. And you know what that means. When you see red, that's when you totally snap and get a spot on the show SNAPPED, and I didn't want that. And besides, I still had to figure out how to get this grown mutherfucker, and apparently broke man, out of my house. But I needed food.

We stopped at the Chinese restaurant, and we walked in. He was still in the best mood. He started talking to the Chinese lady and had the nerve to say some shit in Chinese to her. They started laughing, and then they looked at me. They saw the look on my face (the look of death), then they stopped laughing and got to ordering our food. I sat down, and he sat across from me. He was trying to start a conversation with me but quickly realized that I was in no mood to have any kind of conversation at all with him. I had totally shut down and had nothing left to say. We finally got our food and headed back to the house.

We walked in, and he put the Chinese take-out on the dining room table and said, "Don't worry about the food. I'll bring it in." I answered, "I know, I'm not." And I proceeded to eat. I started feeling better. Ok, look, when I get that hungry, I get borderline violent. You know what I mean. I'm sure I'm not the only one. But then throw in a crazy situation, and we're lucky there wasn't a fatality.

I was sitting at the table eating and

watching him put the groceries away. And as he was doing that, he proceeded to take shit out of my fridge and act like he was cleaning it out. I had to say to him, "Hey, wait a minute. Stop throwing things out, that's not old." It was getting weirder and weirder by the minute. He started spreading paper towels on the counter and putting food on them. I mean, it was just weird. By this point, I gave up. It was getting late, and I was worn out. After I finished eating, I headed upstairs because I was done with this crazy ass day and with Sybil.

I walked into my room, took a shower, and got into bed. I know you are probably wondering if I was nervous about him coming in and trying anything. To be honest, the thought crossed my mind, but that was about it. I really wasn't worried about that because I felt like he knew I wasn't a pushover, and if he tried something, he had better kill me because if he didn't, it would be all bad for him. I really was thinking I just needed to get through this night because tomorrow he was definitely out. He and the 99 cent store he had in my bathroom. Because this shit right here was over. But unfortunately, the nightmare was not quite over just yet.

I don't remember exactly what time I fell asleep, but it was about 3 a.m. I was woken by this strange noise. It sounded like there was a lawnmower in my house. I was trying to remember if it was landscaping day. But I looked at my phone, and it read 3 o'clock in the damn morning, so it was definitely not the landscapers. I sat up and tried to get my bearings. Ok, snap out of it, Bitch, focus. You are at home, and that crazy Sybil muthafucker is downstairs in your house remember? Ok, right, right. I turned and looked at my bedroom door and saw bright lights coming through. Honestly, I didn't know what to think, except why were lights on at 3 o'clock in the morning, and what the fuck was that sound? I walked to my bedroom door and opened it. It was bright as fuck! It seemed like all the lights in the entire house were on. The stairs, the kitchen, and the living room. I mean, every damn light! I needed to find out what was going on in my house.

I started walking down the stairs, and as I got closer to the bottom, I saw Lee VACUUMING the living room carpet! That was the loud noise I was hearing, not a lawnmower. Lol. Ok, but it did sound louder than usual because it was 3 a.m., and the

176

whole city was asleep except this crazy man that was vacuuming my house. I walked down and yelled, "HEY, WHAT IN THE HELL ARE YOU DOING RIGHT NOW? IT'S 3 O'CLOCK IN THE MORNING!!!"

He looked at me and said, "I was just cleaning for you."

"I already did all that before you came. Are you crazy? It's 3 o'clock in the morning!"

He ignored me and kept vacuuming. Ok, right now, I was thinking, ok, I'm gonna leave this one alone right here because NOW I am a little nervous. This is some unstable shit. I didn't say one more word to him. I just turned around and took my ass back up the stairs, went into my room, and locked the door.

That was when I really started to assess my situation. I know, I know, you're thinking, now you're assessing your situation? Well, I didn't know this muthafucker was Sybil crazy before he came. Alright, I just thought he was a little bit of a control freak. And I was just really hoping for the best. But reality had set in, and I was going into survival mode. I was thinking he could be on some kind of drugs or have some kind of PTSD. But really, I didn't give a fuck what was wrong with him. All I could think of was how was I going to get him out of my house with no bloodshed? If this goes sideways, I will not hesitate to domestic violence you!

I was thinking if I called the police, what would I really say. Umm, Officer, yes, I invited this man that I met online but never met in person until now. But we have been talking for six whole months. And I invited him into my house because I thought I really knew him, and we were planning to spend our lives together. I know, STUPID, huh? So much for the blissful seven days I had planned on. Or maybe I would call my ex-husband to come help me get him out. Shit, I could just hear him now. "Wait a minute, let me get this straight. You invited this nigga you never met before to stay with you for a week, and he only gave you $60.00 for the $350 worth of groceries you bought? I would stay too." Ok, never mind. I was definitely not calling him.

I was not calling anyone because I didn't want to escalate the situation, especially if he was on something. I decided to go back to bed and wait it out. I mean, it would be morning in a few hours, and he should be tired by then. That was when we would talk like civilized adults. That was when we would agree that it was just not working, and we should go our separate ways. Right. Crossing my fingers. Alright, that was my plan.

I woke up, and it was now 6 o'clock. Damn, I sure can sleep, can't I? I heard a knock at the door. I opened the door, and he said, "Did you get enough sleep? Remember, no confrontations. I said, "Yes, I did. Did you get any sleep? He said, "Yeah, slept a few hours." I was thinking, ok, that must be some military shit. This man was probably a little fucked up in the head, and I didn't want to find out how fucked up, so I was definitely not going to rock this boat. I was going to just play along.

He went into the bathroom, so I got back into bed because it was only 6 a.m. and who the fuck gets up at 6 a.m. while on vacation? Duh. He came out of the bathroom, and then he walked around the other side of the bed and started to get in. Ok, the reason I got back in bed was I was thinking he would just go back downstairs like he did the night before. Well, that's not what happened this time.

I was turned with my back toward him, and I heard him say, "Are you asleep?" I didn't answer. Then I felt his hand on my back. You know what that means, right?

179

When you're in bed, and you feel a hand on your back, and he starts rubbing it. Whoever you're in bed with, you know that's code for I am horny and in the mood for morning lovin'. I decided I'd had had enough of the Twilight Zone shit. I turned over and said to his face, "This is not happening."

"Oh, come one," he said.

In my most stern voice, I said, "This is not ever going to happen!"

He paused for a minute and then said, "Ok. I am going to change my flight and see what they have."

"Good idea," I said.

He got up and went downstairs.

A few hours later, I was showered and dressed. I headed downstairs, hoping there were no more complications. I saw Lee sitting on the couch.

"I changed my flight, and it leaves at noon," he said.

"Great," I said because I really didn't have any more words.

I went to the kitchen to eat something since I had enough food for a family of 10. But whatever, I didn't want to think about that right now. I wanted to focus on getting him to the airport without incident. I wanted to wait a while before going back upstairs to

180

give him enough time to pack up all his things. The 99 cent store, remember. Think I was more excited that I was getting him out of my house than I was when he first came. I know, sad. He finally came down with his suitcase and bags. I went upstairs to get my purse so we could be on our way. Thank you, Jesus! We were finally on our way back to the airport.

Of course, this was definitely not how I envisioned the last couple of days to go, but that was how it was. As we were driving, I started to feel kind of bad. Don't ask me why because this was some traumatizing shit. Lee was absolutely silent and was looking out the window. We were driving in awkward silence. I felt like I should say something. We reached a stoplight. I turned to him.

"Hey, I'm really sorry this didn't work out," But before I could finish my thought, he interrupted me, and he put his hand up.

"No need to say anything at all." Then he turned his WHOLE body to face out the window.

Well, damn. Forget it then. I was just trying to be nice. Nigga, you lucky I don't throw you out the window with your psycho ass. But ok, ok, I was not going to rock the boat at all. Let me just shut up and quit while I was ahead. And yes, this was me being ahead.

A short ride later, we arrived at the airport. I pulled up to departures, and he departed my car like a bat outta hell and out of my life. Hallelujah! Thank you, Jesus! I made it without involving the police!

Ok, although I am smiling now, this was really not a win. Sure, it was a small victory for me because I still had my life. But I really thought this one was going to be different. Who was I kidding? I knew he was wrong, especially for waiting months before he sent me recent pictures. Because they definitely did not look as good as the ones he had up on his profile. Because they were old pictures. Should have known I wasn't going to get the guy in the pictures on the site. Because that guy did not come to Arizona. I don't know who the guy was who showed up. It was an older ugly muthafucker who wore glasses and didn't tell me he wore glasses.

Yes, I am still salty about that. Lol. I guess I was trying not to judge by looks. But I fuckin' told you that shit don't work, didn't I? If the attraction is not there to begin with, what do we build on? Am I supposed to close my eyes and envision that you are attractive and hope that you will turn me on? Well, that won't work because I will eventually have to open my eyes. So not fair. Not fair at all. Oh well, I tried. Not giving up though. I know my guy is still out there.

CHAPTER NINE: MALE FRIENDS

It was really starting to get frustrating. I was definitely questioning, "Why am I still single? What am I doing wrong here?" It's not like I was going out with #1s. Hell, I don't believe I'm a #1 for a lot of guys. I was picking men I might have things in common and hoped that there was some kind of a spark. Shit, even a flicker we could build on. I really would like some insight on this.

When I talked to my friends, at first, they said, "Well, maybe you are a little too hard on them." But then I shared the full story, then they said, "Oh, Hell, Naw. They deserved everything they got." But are they right? Or are they biased? I honestly feel like I was putting myself out there. I agreed to a date, sometimes, even a second one. But it never failed, they pushed way too hard. If only you would take it easy and try to enjoy our time together instead of acting like it's do or die and go in for the kill. It makes a big difference.

Ok, I am not saying it will always work, but maybe, at the very least, we can remain friends, and who knows what will happen. Am I wrong this? I would love to have male friends in my life. Unfortunately, that is something I have never been able to maintain, a male friendship. Definitely not for lack of trying. I have always been upfront about the type of relationship I believed was happening between me and whomever I met.

For instance, when I was younger, I met a guy out at a party. I gave him my number, but I was completely honest when I told him I was not looking for a relationship right then. I was working on getting my shit together and definitely wasn't looking to get into a relationship, but just someone to hang out with from time to time would be great. He understood, so he said, and agreed that sounded like a great idea. We did that for a little while, probably a month or so. But then I don't know what changed.

One day, after hanging out, I guess he decided to go for it. When we drove up to my place, he tried to kiss me. I don't like confrontations or anything close to them, so I ignored it. But then the muthafucker tried it again. I pulled back and said, "Wait, what are you doing?" He looked at me and said, "I don't just want to be friends with you." Damn. I looked at him and shook my head, got out of the car, and never looked back.

Believe it or not, the same exact thing happened a couple of months later with a different guy. I told him I just wanted to be friends. He agreed and appeared to be fine with it. Until one day, he decided to go for it. Same fuckin' thing. I couldn't understand why nobody wanted to be my friend or why they didn't believe what I said. Well, later, the one male friend I had, told me the truth.

"Unfortunately, Gaby, we will tell you anything to get in the door. Because we really believe that we will be able to change your mind. Especially the more time we spend together."

"Even if I told you from the beginning, I just want to be friends?"

"Yup, even when you tell us that."

Damn, ain't that some shit! Now I know you're asking, "What about this guy? You just said he was your friend, and he seemed to be an honest guy." Well, you're right, he was my friend at that time. But he ended up being and doing the same as all the other so-called friends. The truly sad part about this guy is that I'd known him since I was 19 years old.

Here's what happened with this "friend."

After over a decade of friendship, I guess he said, "Fuck it, I'm going for it." When I thought I could trust him and when I was in a vulnerable state, he showed his Black Ass. It was a night when I'd had too much to drink and knew I could not drive, which, in our younger years, he would always make sure I was ok, and I got home safe. And he NEVER tried anything. I am not the one to drink and drive ever. He offered to put me up in a room not too far from where we were. One of his friends managed the hotel. I was ok with that. I just needed a couple of hours, and I'd be good. And I wasn't falling down drunk but definitely shouldn't drive.

You are probably asking why would you go to a hotel with a man when you were drunk? Well, first of all, I'd known him for many, many years, remember? And second, we had always been just friends, remember? Ok, I knew he liked me, but he had never ever crossed any lines or made me feel uncomfortable. He always made sure I was good. Always. Even when I was in worse condition than this one. I truly trusted him and definitely believed him to be a good friend.

Well, all that shit changed that night. We

got to the room, I went into the bathroom, and when I came out, this Nigga was in his boxers. I ignored him and laid down with all my clothes on, and turned my back to him. Damn, I just wanted to lay my fuckin' head down for a minute. He got in the bed under the covers and tried to push up on me. You know what that means. I'm pretty sure I don't have to spell it out for you. I turned around and looked at him crazy.

"What are you doing?" I yelled.

"Oh, my bad, I'm sorry," he said quickly.

I believe it was because he realized he wasn't going to be able to take advantage of me and the situation.

He got up, put his pants on, and went into the bathroom. I guess he was embarrassed. But shit, why should I have cared about his feelings? What about mine? He shit on our almost two decades old

friendship. I was so furious, I couldn't even sleep. It was about 4:00 a.m.

When he came out of the bathroom, I said, "Take me to my car." On the way back, nothing was really said. We got to my car, I got out of his and into mine. And that was that. I didn't speak to him for years. The crazy part was, whenever I would see him out, he acted like he didn't know why I stopped speaking to him. A grown ass man playing dumb. Needless to say, I have no male friends.

CHAPTER TEN: NOTHERN CALIFORNIA

I figured I would give BPM ONE MORE TRY. After an overwhelming number of messages, I ran across Anthony. He had some nice pictures up. He was tall like 6'3", light-skinned, and handsome. He was medium build, not too big. Just how I like 'em. At least that was what I saw, according to the pictures he had posted. I was interested, so I sent him a message. I really liked his pictures, so I was excited to start a conversation.

Later that afternoon, he responded to my message. We went back and forth messaging then we exchanged numbers, so we didn't have to continue communicating on the site. Our first telephone conversation went very well. He was pretty outgoing and witty and funny. I liked it. He thought the same about me — the witty and funny part. Especially when I shared a few dating stories with him.

I had him laughing. He then shared a few of his stories, and we had a good laugh. I was happy that our initial conversation went better than I expected.

We did the same thing every night for a week. I was really enjoying myself, and he told me the feeling was mutual. Thanksgiving was the following week, and I was thankful for meeting Anthony. I was very hopeful that better days were on the horizon. Since things were going great, I believed it was time to talk about meeting in person.

Every year I take my one-week vacation the week of my birthday, which is December 29. The next time we talked, I brought up just that. He suggested that I take my vacation in Northern Cali that year. I was already way ahead of him. I just was letting him say it first. You know, so I didn't look like a hoebag who did that all the time, which I don't.

"Ok, that sounds like a good idea. Are you sure?

I don't want you to be uncomfortable," he said.

"I am totally sure. This should be a great time."

We were getting along really well. We had a lot in common. We liked to joke, and he kept me laughing, which I love. I had sent him pictures because, you know, I wanted him to have recent pictures of me.

"So, where's my picture(s)?" I asked him one night.

"Ok, I'll send you one, no problem," he told me. After we finished our call, I got a text. It said, "Selfie I just took." Was I nervous? Hell yeah! Because I didn't want it to change the vibe that we were having. And you know how I feel about looks and attraction. Ok...ok... I know what you're saying, "Bitch, just open the text!" Ok, ok. Damn, you guys are pushy.

I opened the text with the picture, and it definitely looked like he literally just took it. No preparation, not trying to fix himself up or nothing. Well, damn. He was in a plain t-shirt and pajama bottoms. Alright, this was what it was right at this moment. I will not lie to you. I was a little disappointed. He was a little heavier and a little lighter up top than in the pictures he had on the site. I had to say something, so I just said, "Ok, cool, thank you." I know guys don't like sending selfies, so I did appreciate the pic. But what I was thinking was, I don't appreciate you looking like you stayed home from work because you have the flu. But I didn't say that.

The next day, I went to work and had to show my co-worker because I had to get a second opinion on it. I had already told her about him when we first started talking, so she knew what was going on. I mentioned to her that I got a selfie from Anthony.

"And?" she asked.

I showed it to her. Then I pulled up the website and showed her the pictures he had posted. I told her how I was feeling about it and the differences that were obvious. I mean, she understood what my concerns were. Who knows how recent the pictures were, but let me tell you what I saw. He was noticeably thinner on the website pictures. Not that he was 50 pounds heavier in the selfie, just definitely heavier. Also, the thinning hair thing. I'm not saying he was suddenly George Jefferson, but let's just say he was on his way there, and from the looks of the selfie, he was getting there sooner rather than later. I said maybe the lighting was bad. And you know, guys don't give a shit how they look before they send a picture. For example, I will take 15 to 20 pictures to get five decent ones, and out of those five, only two look good to me. I get it, guys aren't going to do all that. But damn, maybe you should have taken a little time to get dressed. You know, because we've never even met yet. Because this really tells me you give two fucks about how you look, and what I think about your appearance.

My friend said she got what I was saying, but he didn't look that bad.

"I don't think he can look any worse than this shit, right?" I asked.

"Right," she agreed.

Ok, I felt better. Let us forget this ever happened because if I ever looked at that picture again, I was going to throw the WHOLE phone in the trash. Alright, I got over the selfie thing, and we continued talking every night. We were counting down until my flight to San Francisco.

The day I fly out to finally meet Anthony has arrived. I am going to be in the Bay area for 11 whole days! It could either go great or be a total disaster, and hopefully, they find my body at least, so I could have a proper burial. But I was not thinking anything but good thoughts. Ok, here we go.

I touched down in San Francisco on a Thursday night. I got there and found my way out of the airport and quickly found out that the cute leather jacket

I had on felt like I had nothing on. It was

freezing! I had no idea it got this cold out here. I mean, it is California. I am from Southern California, and it ain't nothing like this. I was standing outside, waiting for Anthony, trying not to die. I had already texted him I was here, so I was just waiting for him to pull up. I am not exaggerating about how cold it was out there. It was like 40 to 45 degrees in this bitch! Definitely not used to this weather at all. But right now, all I could think about was how is this going to go?

Anthony said he was almost to me. I told him what I was wearing, and he spotted me. Alright, that's him in a Nissan Altima. Ok, cool. He had a hat on and not a baseball hat. One of those cool hats that guys wear. I think they're called driver's caps. He had jeans on and a jacket. I think they're called bubble jackets. I mean, he looked pretty cool. And tall. Like 6'3". I know you're asking, so what number is he? He was a #1. He looked like his pictures but aged. I think the pictures weren't that current, but it was definitely him. He looked at me and said, "That little jacket is not going to keep you warm." With a laugh, he went to his trunk and pulled out another jacket for me to put on and some gloves. I looked at him and said, "Bless you, my child." He laughed and called me crazy.

We arrived at Fisherman's Warf, and I was so ready to get some food because I was starving. He said, "Ok, let's get some grub!" We found a spot to get shrimp and clam chowder soup. I love me some clam chowder soup. I was in heaven. Nothing fancy, just a low-key spot to sit and eat. We weren't really talking much, just eating. Once we were done, we disposed of our trash and decided to go walking. I know what you're thinking. I thought you said it was freezing out there. And it definitely was. But he gave me an extra jacket and gloves, remember, so I was good. At least for a little while, then I'd have to thaw out inside somewhere.

He was from San Francisco, so he knew the area well. He told me about when they used to come to this area back in the day. He told me there used to be a club around here, but it was gone now. He was strolling down memory lane, and I was happy to listen.

We finally decided to make our way back to the car. I know you're wondering what I was thinking. How was I feeling about him? Well, at that moment I was totally happy. He really was a man's man. He took charge and was taking good care of me. Because if we hadn't gotten back to the car, I would have totally frozen.

We were now on our long journey to his house in Modesto. I had no idea where that was or how far. It was about 10:30 p.m., and I was kind of worn out. I worked until early afternoon, then caught a flight out, walked the cold streets on Fisherman's Warf, and I was pretty exhausted. He said, "Go ahead and lay back because it's about an hour and a half drive back home." I said, "Holy shit." I tried to stay up as long as I could, but after a while, it was lights out for me.

I finally felt the car making some turns, and I woke up to FOG! Lots and lots of fog! I sat up and looked around. He saw this deer in headlights look I had and said, "It's ok. It gets like this in the winter." OMG it was crazy. I mean, you couldn't see shit. I mean, nothing. I was scared. All I could think of was, what if a car comes? We won't be able to see each other. Damn, I should have stayed asleep. I couldn't sleep anymore, and I was starting to feel the panic building up inside of me. But before I could lose it and make a total jackass of myself, we turned off on some street, and he said we're almost there. Thank you, sweet Jesus!

We arrived, and he quickly sent me into the house while he got my things out of the

197

car. Ok, Mr. Gentleman. I definitely liked that. Alright, people, nothing happened that night. I was still thawing out, and I was exhausted. We slept in the same bed, but he was a perfect gentleman and let me sleep. Damn, y'all nasty.

The next morning was my birthday! He was already up before I even woke up. I opened my eyes and saw him in front of me with a bowl of fruit and orange juice. He said, "Good morning and Happy Birthday to you!" I looked at him, and I said, "Thank you. Aren't you sweet." For those of you who don't know me, I am not really a morning person. Not that I'm like Scrooge or anything, I just am kind of quiet for a while until I fully wake up. That's all.

But Mr. Anthony, on the other hand, seemed to definitely be a morning person. He was quite cheerful that I kind of made fun of him. I told him, "Why, thank you, Benson. I appreciate the fruit." He laughed because he knew exactly what I was talking about. See, we had the same humor. Definitely a good sign. He saw me and quickly realized that I was not quite ready to get up, and he said, "Why don't you go back to sleep. It's still early, and you are going to need all your energy because I have a full day planned for us today."

"Ok, good idea," I said.

A couple of hours later, I was ready to get the day started. I ate some of the fruit he'd left on the table for me, oranges and bananas cut up into small pieces. That was very thoughtful of him. He told me to dress comfortably because we were going to be doing a lot of walking. An hour later, I was dressed and ready to go. Let's get this party started!

Alright, we were driving down to San Francisco for the day. On the ride, he told me how he was really into Reggae music and not the dance reggae—reggae music with a message. And with that being said, I learned all about the difference for over an hour. We were finally off the freeway, and we pulled off into a residential area. I didn't ask any questions. I was just observing the area. Basically, just in case it ended up being a kidnapping, I could find my way out or give a description of where I was. You know, 48 Hours type shit. He found parking on some street. It looked like a nice area and pretty peaceful.

"Ok, we're here," he said.

I was looking around thinking, he didn't say we were going to someone's house. I kept my mouth shut and let him lead. Hopefully, not to my death because I kept my mouth shut. We started walking on the sidewalk that led to the back of houses, but it was a very narrow trail. A dirt trail full of trees and bushes. It looked like some kind of hiking trail. I was thinking, ok, he wouldn't be dumb enough to kill me in the middle of the day. Would he? Ok, then I was pretty confident I wouldn't be dying because there were more people walking on this trail.

After walking for a minute, we came to a broader area that had a lot of very steep steps. But every so often, while walking up the steps, there was a bench to the right. I was assuming for anyone who needed a rest. I suddenly realized we were on a hike. Well, I'll be damned. I was hiking. Even though I always said I didn't do hiking. During one of our conversations, I do remember him asking me if I hiked. I told him I did not hike because I didn't want to get eaten by mountain lions or bitten by snakes. And I had definitely never been interested in mountain hiking or anything like that.

As we were walking, every so often, he asked me how I was doing. For the most part, I was doing ok until we reached another set of long steep steps. He looked at me and said, smiling, "Ok, let's take a break and sit down on this bench coming up to the right." I had this look on my face, a cross between wow, this is pretty amazing and sweet Jesus, please helicopter me out of here because I'm not gonna make it. He turned to me and asked how I was doing. I was thinking, I am so glad I ate something because I definitely would have fallen out by now. I told him, "I am actually ok. I think I am doing pretty good. I am really proud of myself right now." He agreed with me. He told me previously that he walked miles every day when he got off the train to get to his job site, so I knew he was a walking and hiking machine.

So, what was I thinking and feeling right now? I was actually loving it. It was something different than I was used to, so I was loving it. He then said, "We don't have much further to go. Then we'll get to the cliff." Umm, say what. A cliff? Ok, I guess this is where I die. Lol. We made it up the last set of steep steps and got to a wide area where there were people scattered around. We kept walking, and as we got closer to the cliff, I suddenly saw the ocean. Well, I'll be damned. He took me on a hike, and we ended up on a cliff overlooking the ocean. It was a magnificent view.

We stopped and took it in. He was standing next to me, and he put his arm around me. I was thinking, yes, this was going really well. I was enjoying his company, and he was enjoying mine. What I noticed about him was that he seemed to be protective and nurturing. Or at least he was being that way with me, and I was loving that. On the way back down was not a problem for me. I loved to see so many people getting their exercise this way.

We were now starving, so we found a place to have a light lunch. Nothing elaborate, just a place where we could relax and be together and learn more about each other. It was really nice being out eating and drinking because we had no place to be. I loved it. Oh, and did I mention he also smoked reefer. Lol. He had asked me if I did. I told him I did not, but I didn't mind if he did. I grew up in the hood, remember. It was not a big deal to me.

The sun had set, and he wanted to take me somewhere overlooking the city. We got to this small parking lot on an uneven street. It's kind of hidden away. At night, if you don't know where you are going, you won't find it. But if you do find it, it is a hidden gem. All the city lights and the stars — it is a spectacular view. What made it even better was how well we were getting along. It was now about 7 p.m., and he told me our dinner reservation wasn't until 9, so he wanted to take me to a place where we could have drinks. Sounded good to me.

We drove for about 30 minutes or so. Then we were driving down a few streets until he finally said, "Ok, I think this is it." We were in a residential area, or at least that's what it looked like in the dark. Off to the left, there was a small parking lot where we parked. We got out, and he went in the trunk to give me his extra jacket because it had gotten pretty cold again. We headed down a walkway, and it looked like over to the far left was a golf course. But it was really dark. I mean, dark enough that if he wanted to kill me, this would have been a perfect place for it to happen. I mean, there was no one in sight. The more we walked, the more I was thinking, damn, after the great day I just had, this is how it all ends for me. Welp, at least he showed me a good time before he ended my life. Ok, ok, ok. I snapped out of it when he said, "There it is. That's what I was looking for."

As we were walking, I started to see more clearly that we were now on the grounds of the Ritz Carlton Hotel. Now, I've been to a few of these hotels. There is one in Phoenix. But the one in Orange County is a pretty nice one. But this one was pretty spectacular overlooking the ocean. As we walked up, there was a huge Christmas tree beautifully lit up so bright. Off to the left, there were a couple of fire pits with chairs. There were a few couples enjoying the fire pits and the view. We found a spot, and he said, "I'm going to go inside and get some drinks." And off he went.

I was taking it all in. The beautiful landscaped grounds, flowers, bushes, and this was all overlooking the ocean at the bottom of the cliff. It was very dark except for the fire pits and the hotel lights. Oh, and the gigantic Christmas tree. And then there was the sound of the ocean. Man, it was pretty amazing. I had to admit, he was pretty smooth, this guy. Before I could finish my thought, he came with our drinks. We toasted it up and enjoyed the ambiance. Then he pulled his phone out and put on some R&B music for us to listen to. See, smooth. We were sitting very close, and he had his arm around me. Mainly because if we didn't huddle up, we would very quickly develop hyperthermia. Not even kidding. But the alcohol was warming me up.

After a while, it was time to be on our way to dinner. As we got on the path back to the car, he grabbed my hand and said, let's go this way. So, we went straight instead of staying on the path the way we came. Ok, I take it back, this was where it would all end for me because it was dark as hell out there, and not a soul in sight. Well, at least it was on these beautiful grounds and not in an alley that stank of urine. As we walked, I started to see a cliff and then the ocean. Damn, another spectacular ocean view. And let me tell you, the ocean at night is even more amazing than in the day. It's just mesmerizing. He got behind me, wrapped his arms around me, and everything in the whole world stopped, and it was only the two of us and the ocean. He let go of me, and I turned to face him. This was where we had our first kiss. That was some shit out of one of my romance novels. Before I could think too much about it, he grabbed my hand and said, "Come on, we have to go. Our reservation is at 9."

In the car, he told me we were going to Morton's for a good steak. Perfect because I love me some good meat. Pun intended. When we got there, it was crowded, and I quickly realized we didn't have reservations. Not really sure why he said we did when we clearly did not. We waited for 45 damn minutes! But honestly, I didn't even mind because it gave us more time to talk. Finally, I heard them call his name, and they showed us to our table. I was so hungry, I could barely see. I ate so much, I was literally about to pass out. No really, waiting for the bill, I could barely keep my eyes open. Then right when I was about to drop my head on the table, the waiter came. Whew, just in the nick of time before total embarrassment.

Anthony knew how tired I was. As soon as we got in the car, he said, "Man, you had a full day, huh? Just put your seat back and relax." I know, sweet, huh? I don't even remember the ride back. All I remember is waking up in the bed for a minute, thinking, wow, did this just happen? And I answered myself, "Yes...Yes, it fuckin' did." And I went right back to sleep.

I finally woke up the next morning. Well, it was barely morning. It was 11 a.m.! Damn, I didn't realize it was that late. What woke me up was music. Yup, you guessed it. Reggae Music! Tonight, he was taking me to see a live band at a jazz club. We decided not to really do too much and hung out at the house. He asked me if I played dominoes, and I told him, "No, I don't know how to play." That was the day he taught me how to play dominoes. He said, "Oh, you goan learn today!"

I was having the best time. We were drinking, he was smoking, and then dominoes. What's better than that? Evidently, he was a pretty good teacher because I started winning games, and he was no longer taking it easy on me. Ahh, good times.

Later that night, we hit the club, and both shows were sold out. We had a great time and then headed back home. Well, not my home, his home. You know what I mean. I know you are wondering if this was the night that IT happens? Right, that's what you're wondering? Nope, not yet. Not that night. He was a perfect gentleman. So much so, I was beginning to question if he was attracted to me at all. We were definitely having a fantastic time, but he never tried anything once it was time to go to bed. Hmmm, could I be reading this all wrong? Well, I decided this was the day to bring it up. It was day 4.

He had planned for us to go on a wine train in Napa that day. I woke up again to my bowl of fruit and juice on the nightstand.

Damn, I could really get used to this. I was wondering if he was doing this for show. You know, only in the beginning, and then it dies off to nothing. I hate when that happens. I mean, I get that you always try to put your best foot forward, but damn, it doesn't mean you have to completely stop being thoughtful. Does it? I believe the only reason you stop is that it is totally out of character for you to be that way, and that really sucks. To know that you can't even be thoughtful without being asked to be. Anyway, let's get back to my day.

We got to the train in Napa, and the inside of the train was absolutely beautiful. It was like an old train from the 50s. I felt like we should have gotten dressed up. I totally loved it. We had appetizers, wine, and a five-course meal. I had the best time, again.

Now we were back at the house and settled in and relaxed. Again, he got out the massage oil for my foot massage. Oh, I forgot to tell you, every night, he got out his special foot massage oil and gave me a little foot massage. I know, I was getting the red-carpet treatment. After my foot massage, we busted out the dominoes. Then the drinking and then the smoking began. We were having a party, a party for two. And it was just perfect.

Don't get me wrong, we had a spat. It was a disagreement that could have easily turned ugly had it not been for communication. It was over something silly, but because he wasn't used to having another opinion to consider in a very long time, he totally dismissed what I was saying. But then he stopped, thought about it, and got it. I could literally see his wheels turning. Afterward, he said, "You know what, you are right. I do need to consider how you are feeling and not ignore that." And just like that, the situation de-escalated and was done. Now, back to our party of two.

In the middle of our dominoes game, I decided that this was the time for our conversation. You know the one about adult relations.

"So, is there a reason why you haven't tried anything? Like touching me. I mean, it's ok if you're not interested," I began.

"I just didn't want to be pushy. I wanted it to just happen organically. It's definitely not because I don't want you. So, let me show you."

With that being said, he took me by the hand and into the bedroom. And... this is where I let you use your imagination.

The days and nights rolled by, and it was

time for me to head back home to Arizona and get back to reality. I had to admit, this was the best initial meeting I'd ever had. All I could think about was how I wished it didn't have to end. Don't you hate that? Especially when you are having a good time. Before I left, we definitely talked about making plans to get together again very soon.

After a couple of weeks, I made a trip back and had a great visit filled with drinking, smoking, and more dominoes. Oh, and some good ole relations as well. Next month was Valentine's Day, so I made plans to make it back to California. Things were going very well with us. We talked just about every night and had good conversations when we did. We were also texting regularly.

The plan was for me to fly down Friday. Valentine's Day was on Saturday, and I'd stay until Sunday. Ok, time to catch my flight to go see my man. BTW, during our conversations, he was telling me how he was done dating and done searching. He had found his girl. How he wanted me to move there so we could start our lives together. Well, all sounds good, right? But slow down there, cowboy. I have a WHOLE life back in Arizona, so that will take some time. But definitely a nice thought.

It was now Valentine's Day, and love was in the air. I got him a gift and a card, you know, because it was Valentine's Day. Before we left for the day, I gave him his gift and card. He opened the small box and pulled out a black set of dominoes. I custom ordered a set because I knew how he loved dominoes, and that set was much nicer than the one we had been playing with. He really liked them. He thanked me, kissed me, and put the card on the mantle.

You're probably wondering what he got me, right? And the answer to that is nothing. Ok, look. I didn't get him something, so he would get me something. However, did I expect to get something, anything on Valentine's Day from the man I had been in a relationship with for 3 months? Yes. I kind of did. But damn, not even a card. Ok, whatever. Maybe he thought since he was taking me out, that was the same thing. What do you think? Should I have expected anything? Was taking me out equivalent to a gift on Valentine's Day? Whether a man thinks Valentine's Day is not a real thing or not, if your girl does, then I believe you should at least try to put a smile on her face. Not this guy. He didn't even give it a second thought. Didn't even say, "I didn't get you anything."

At dinner, I was thinking, is this petty of me to be still thinking about this? In my mind, it made me wonder about future special occasions—if he would ignore them too. And if you're thinking maybe he didn't do Valentine's Day. That's not it because he had brought it up in our previous conversations, and he was just as excited as I was that we would be together on the lover's day. For him to not acknowledge it at all anymore while I was live and in person caused me a little bit of pause.

At dinner, he talked about our future together and even marriage. I am not saying I didn't feel the same about him, I'm just saying it had only been three months. We'd spent a total of seventeen days together. Just putting things into perspective. Everything was going great, but it was supposed to be in the beginning. I mean, I don't know if he scratched his ass in his sleep or if he farted and how bad the smell was, and maybe I couldn't stomach it. And more importantly, I hadn't seen him when he was angry. Shit, he hadn't seen me when I was angry either. And since it was a long-distance relationship, it was going to take some time. Well, I do know that his draws weren't dirty because while he was at work, I'd done his laundry. Come on, don't act like you've never done some inspections of your own. Lol.

March was his birthday, and I wanted to plan to be there so we could spend it together. I bought my ticket as usual. I was trying to figure out what to get him for his birthday. I didn't want to get the usual like cologne or clothes. Besides, I didn't know his size, and if I asked him now, he would know what I was up to. I was surfing the web for ideas, and I ran across a website with a bunch of love gifts. A lot of poems, inscriptions on watches, shirts, things of that nature. Then I saw something interesting. A message in a bottle that was in a treasure box to fit the bottle. There were different messages you could choose from, or you could send in your own words, and they would inscribe it on old 1950s paper, roll it up, and put it in the bottle. You get the picture. I know it's very sappy, but I liked it.

Ok, let me tell you how things were with us at this point. I had come down a couple of weeks before for his grandmother's funeral. That was pretty rough. But I had to make sure I was there, like anyone would for someone they cared about, right. I met some of his family and his kids. I think it went well under the circumstances. But before that, I had noticed that he didn't really want to get out like we used to the last times I'd been down. Not really sure why. We hadn't been dating that long for the honeymoon to be over yet. It had only been 21 days we had spent together. San Francisco was still very new to me. When I flew out there, I still wanted to see the city. There was still so much for me to see. I knew this wasn't a big deal to him because he lived there, but it was a big deal to me. We were still getting to know each other, but things were still good.

Alright, it was time to catch my flight to San Francisco. Friday night, he picked me up from the airport, and he took me to a seafood restaurant nearby. This was the second time we'd been there. A really nice place and delicious seafood. I noticed quietness between us.

Ok, let me just tell you where my head was at. In a previous conversation, he'd told me he was leaving early from work to pick me up. And the day before, he told me he was going to bring a change of clothes because he was not going to drive all the way home and then come all the way back, which made total sense. Well, when he picked me up. This time he parked and met me inside the airport instead of driving by like he had every other time. Not sure why he came inside this time, but ok, great. When I saw him, he was dressed like he just came from work and didn't change clothes. Or maybe he did? He had a polo shirt on and jeans and he was tucked in up to his neck with what looked like work boots. When I saw him, I was wondering if he was going to change before we went to dinner. The reason why I bring this up is because we were going to this nice restaurant and what he had on was super casual, not really appropriate for this restaurant. Maybe he thought because he was tucked in real tight, it made him look better. But no, it did not. You still look like you should be going to a bar or Chinese takeout because you just got off work. You get my point. Right.

The restaurant wasn't crowded, but there were people, and I saw them kind of looking my way. Alright, maybe I am being a little bougie right now, but shit, why didn't you just do what you said you were going to do? Now there was this awkward silence while we waited for our food to come because I was a little disappointed. Why can't people just do what they say they are going to do? Anyway, we got through dinner and got on the road for the long ride to Modesto. I was so ready for a good night's sleep.

The next morning was a gloomy, rainy day. I walked into the kitchen, and Anthony was fixing breakfast. I walked up behind him and gave him a big hug.

"Good morning and Happy Birthday to you, mister! How are you feeling today?"

"I'm feeling real good. Thanks, babe."

I went back into the room and got his gift and card. I yelled out, "I got you something, baby!" I handed it to him, and he sat it on the table. I looked at him, and I said, "Open it now!" He looked at me and smiled.

"Ok. Ok," he said. "This is beautiful. I love it." He gave me a kiss and went back to cooking breakfast. Definitely not the reaction I was expecting. I mean, I wasn't expecting cartwheels or anything. But that seemed like a brush off. Like it was not a big deal when, in fact, it was a big deal. I put a lot of thought into that gift. He didn't even read the message in the muthafuckin' bottle! I know what you're saying. "Maybe he's not a sensitive guy and really isn't into stuff like that." Well, yes, he is. We'd had conversations and watched a bunch of romantic movies (chick flicks). So, yes, he did like stuff like this. But you know what? Fuck it, I was done with it.

I asked him if he felt like getting out. He said, not really. He was cool with just kicking it at home. Ok with me, too, because it was whatever-Anthony-wanted-to-do day. So, drinking and smoking it was. That is exactly what we did. Dominoes, Reggae music, alcohol, and smoking all day til we dropped. Literally. Oh, and a little bit of sexual relations as well. I say little because the only time we did IT was while we were playing, and the winner got whatever he or she wanted. He won and wanted some lovin. It was short but sweet. But never did I think that was the only time I was going to be getting some. But it was. It started to be a pattern and not a good one. Maybe it was an old thing, he was over 50. 52 to be exact.

The next morning was Sunday, my last day there. When I woke up, Anthony was nowhere to be found. I got up and started to search the house. He was not in the kitchen or the living room. I went downstairs, and there he was, curled up on a recliner.

"Hey, why are you down here?" I asked.

"Oh, I just came down here to watch some movies. I didn't want to wake you," he said.

I looked at him with a confused look on my face, and said, "You've never woken me up before. But, ok."

He was in a recliner covered up with a blanket, so it was not like I could lay with him. Kind of strange. Especially because he was making no effort to include me in whatever he was doing. My flight was later that evening, so this was definitely not how I wanted to spend our last day together. Alright, dude. I'm going to leave it alone and go back upstairs. It's freezing down in this cave.

Later that day, we left to catch my flight. We decided to stop for a late lunch at a spot close to the airport. During that outing, he started asking me random questions. Like if I ever wanted to get married again. How I liked it on this side of California since I was from Southern California and not Northern. Then he didn't really say too much after that.

After we ate, we still had a little time to kill before we needed to head to the airport, so we decided to take a walk on this trail that was right outside the restaurant. During that walk, it had gotten even more awkward. He was not really his normal talkative self. And honestly, I was not really in the mood to play 21 questions to find out why. He was holding my hand during our walk, so I didn't see anything wrong with just enjoying the walk.

After about an hour, it was time to head to the airport. He parked and he walked me in to see me off. Once we got to the checkpoint, he gave me a hug and a kiss and told me to let him know when I got back to Arizona. Once I touched down in Phoenix, I sent him a quick text letting him know I made it back safe and sound.

Once I got back home, I relaxed for the rest of the night and got ready for work in the morning.

I was woken up at about 5 a.m. by a text. I looked at the phone, and it was Anthony. It was a very long text. I started reading, and it started off with, "Well, after much consideration..." WTF is this?! Who am I, a colleague? SMH. Ok, is this a joke? Am I being punked right now? Even though I normally don't wake up til 7 a.m., I was wide awake. You have got to be kidding me? Was this a Dear John letter? The more I read, the worse I felt. My heart literally almost stopped. I don't know about you, if you've ever experienced anything like this before, but for me it feels like I just caught the flu. I instantly felt so sick to my stomach like my whole body was starting to ache. I didn't even really know what was happening. Neither did my body. The more I read, it became a clearer that, yes, this was a Dear John letter. Well, a Dear John text. Not sure which is worse. I think they are both equally fucked up. I couldn't even believe what I was reading. He said he felt I was never in it, and I didn't put much effort into the relationship. WHAT!!! So, all the times I flew there and spent my money and took time off work and my life for us to be together, that didn't count? This mutherfucker never came to see me. You have got to be kidding me? He went on to say I hadn't reciprocated his feelings and that all I cared about was going out. And the time I was there when his grandmother died, I was inconsiderate because I wanted to go out, and I should have understood how he was feeling. Ok, that was kind of fucked up that he would even throw that in my face.

First of all, the day of the funeral, he was pretty up beat the whole day. I understand that people grieve in different ways but what he was showing me was that he was ok and not a basket case. And I thought that maybe we should be out instead of sitting at home. I thought sitting at home would make him feel worse. It was not because I was ignoring the situation and wanted to go out and have a good time. And that's exactly what happened. He sat in his reclining chair and went to sleep until I left. But, ok, whatever. I guess that was how he took it. Why he didn't bring it up back then, I don't know, or any time before now was some bullshit.

The other main point he wanted me to know, and this is for my very adult readers, was the fact that I hadn't reciprocated fellatio. Yes, he used that specific word. In other words, as Bernie Mac would say, I didn't put my mouth on him. Ok, look, I don't know if there is anyone out there that will agree or understand what I am going to say, but this is my explanation of this very adult topic of oral sex. I do not have a problem with giving or receiving oral sex or "fellatio" as he put it. The older I have gotten, I have grown to love it. With the right person, of course. I mean, I don't just go around sucking random dick or letting any old body lick or suck on my pussy. What I am saying is, I am not opposed to giving or receiving it. I know what you're saying, "Alright, bitch, get to the point." Ok, Ok. Here is what I'm trying to say.

We did not have sex often. I mean, it wasn't like we were fucking like rabbits. I've done that before when you are so sexually attracted to someone and you are just turned on all the time, so you have sex, a lot. This was not that. But the times we did have sex, it was more like him going down on me. And if I'm being perfectly honest, he was kind of a little too rough for me. I mean, my shit is sensitive, and he was like an animal that was starving, and my pussy was the food. Way too much for her and me. Then he immediately came up, opened my legs and boom sex. And then it was over. Didn't last all that long either. Definitely not long enough for him to pause so I could suck his dick and then continue fucking. Nope, that never happened. All the times we started, it was just that fast, so he never gave me a chance to start off. It was always he went straight downtown, and I didn't want to stop him to tell him it was too rough, and it wasn't doing anything for me. So, I just let him. But shit, looking back, I think if I would have sucked his dick, that would have been all she wrote, if you know what I mean.

Does this make any sense to anyone? Alright, all that being said, he still had one last complaint. He brought up the one time he told me he loved me. He said I couldn't even say it back. The one and only time he said it goes like this.

We were having a good time. We had just enjoyed a day full of drinking, smoking, and playing dominoes. We moved it into the bedroom. We were kissing, he took my clothes off, and he took his clothes off. He laid me on the edge of the bed, and then he was inside of me. Then he stopped and just looked at me and said, "You are such a beautiful creature." Then in the midst of that, he said, while he was still inside of me, "I love you." I will admit, it totally caught me off guard. I just kissed him, and then he finished.

Look, I don't just say I Love You to anyone unless I mean it. Not even to not hurt your feelings. And I certainly didn't want to say it because you said it to me during sex. Clearly, his feelings were hurt for him to even bring that up. I mean, it's not like he told me he loved me in a normal conversation or ever brought it up after that time. So, this fuckin' Dear John letter made no sense. I believed since he thought I didn't love him, he figured he would break up with me first. I just want to say, just because I didn't say I love you right at that moment didn't mean I don't care about you, and my feelings weren't growing. Because they were. But I guess not fast enough for him.

Right now, I was totally hurt, sad, and heartbroken. Because all this time and effort, poof, gone. I know you're saying, "Just call him and talk to him." Uhh, duh. I tried that, but he did not answer the 10 times I called him. Nothing worse than being ignored when you just got earth-shattering news. And there is nothing you can do about it. It's not like I could show up at his door. Oh, and get this, I had already bought a ticket to go down there the following weekend. But did he put in his text that he would reimburse me for my ticket? No, he did not. Oh, wait a minute, I think he did. But did he? Nope. But I didn't care about that. We were supposed to be in a grownup relationship. You know, because one of us was over 50 fuckin' years old!

We made future plans. He wanted me to move there and many other things he said he wanted for us. All I could do was cry and go over our whole relationship in my head, trying to figure out what I missed. Sad huh? You get hurt, and all you can do is think about what you could've done differently and what you can do to try and fix it. But there is nothing you can do when the other person won't even talk to you. I had to take the day off to be alone and just cry and try to pick myself back up. Nothing worse than unexpected bad news.

Right. Especially when you didn't even

see it coming. Not one clue. I mean, this mutherfucker walked me to the gate, and then I even talked to him while I was waiting to board my flight. So, NO, I didn't see this one coming at all. At the very least, I thought if he ever had a problem, he would talk about it because he always said it was all about communication. Lying sack of shit! Even if you did have any complaints, I certainly did not deserve to be treated like this. And yet here I am. I was left with having to try and figure out how to pick up the pieces and move on. How did I even get here... again?

Man, every day was rough for a while. Months went by until I was finally ready to get back on that muthafuckin horse. Well, I wasn't really ready. I had to force myself because I refused to let him get the best of me. It took a little self-motivation at times. I told myself, look, Bitch, get up, stand up. He does not deserve your tears. He wasn't even good in bed. He definitely did not fit the stereotype of big hands and big feet. If you know what I mean, and I know you do. But it would be really petty of me to spell everything out, so I won't. He does not deserve you. He was selfish and only thought about himself, and you know it. So, get up and be the bad bitch that you are!

225

Well, damn. I couldn't even be depressed in my own head. Lol. But thank the Lord for my strong inner bitch, right. Because I was really heartbroken. I really believed the reason why it had been so hard to let go and move on was because of those first 11 days we spent together. I mean, I've had relationships before. But what I am saying is that I'd never had a better first meeting of 11 consecutive days with anyone before. I guess that was what I was holding on to. Even though everyone kept telling me, "Let go of that shit. He doesn't deserve you at all." I know, I know. At least my head knew that. But my heart was still down in the dumps. All I can say is this one took me a while to get over. After months went by, he reached out. And stupid me, I listened to what he had to say. I went back and tried it again. We went back and forth a couple more times. But each time it was the same ole shit. Him pulling back with his self-serving reasons. So, finally, I got it. This was not the man for me. My inner self was telling me, "Hey dumb, dumb, how many times are you going to let him keep treating you like this before walking away? This man is showing you what he thinks about you by flip-flopping back and forth with your life." OK, I FINALLY

GET IT! That's me yelling back at myself. And FINALLY, that was the end of Anthony and country ass Modesto.

CHAPTER ELEVEN: TINDER DATING

Ok, after a little break from men, it was time to get back on that damn horse. And not the same horse. This was a different horse because the other one I beat to death, remember. Come on, keep up with me. Ok, it was time to see what this Tinder dating I kept seeing everywhere was all about. I needed to find out what all that swipe righting meant.

I signed myself up, created a profile, and posted some pictures, recent pictures and not from 1999. My opening line was short and sweet: "Good Vibes Only." So, I started to swipe, a lot of lefts, I started seeing the number of men swiping right for me going up. I checked them out and what I noticed on this particular site was that the eligible dating pool had gotten a lot bigger/better from the previous sites I had been on. What I mean is that on here, I was finding a lot more men who had established careers like doctors, lawyers, pilots, athletes — just a larger variety and better-looking men as well. So I say, let the games begin! I was actually excited and looking forward to a little fun. Please, Lord Jesus, keep the crazies, weirdos, and stalkers away.

On this site, there were some Blacks... excuse me, African Americans... and Mexicans but mainly Whites, probably 75% to 80%. And most of my swipe righters were uh... White. So, you know what, I decided to give White a try. I mean, shit, I hadn't had much luck with the non-whites. So, what the hell.

Date

Ted was older than me, like 8 years older. He was an Arizona local. We messaged a bit, then we exchanged numbers. During our telephone conversation, we set up a date to meet in a couple of days. We decided on a restaurant closer to me than him. I got to the restaurant, and it was on the high end side and very white. Whenever I went there, I seemed to get stares and looks. And honestly, I'm not exactly sure what they were all about. The obvious reason is that I am not White. I am a light-skinned, biracial woman. But I would like to think that maybe the other reason is that I am an attractive woman. Maybe it's a little bit of both, and I'm ok with that. I mean, I've gotten this all my life, so definitely nothing new to me. And, as a matter of fact, old white men seem to love me.

Short story: I worked with this girl at a law firm, of course, where everyone was white, including Amy. But she was a real cool ass white girl who I would go to lunch with just about every day. We talked about a lot of things, work, men, you know, everything. On this particular day, we were headed to lunch when on our way out, an attorney from down the hall stopped us. He asked if I had a particular law book because he was looking for some case law. I told him, "Yes, you can go right in and grab what you need." Amy then said she was going to the bathroom, and she'd be right back. I waited for her in front of our office. When the attorney came back outside, I turned to face him, and I found him staring at me. He said to me, "I was wondering if we could exchange numbers so I can take you out sometime?"

Ok, this totally caught me off guard. Sometimes, men that I would never think are interested in me, I find out are. This was one of those times. The reason why I say that is he was an older, white man in his 60's. I was in my 30's. He was tall and thin, and he looked like he could've been a good-looking man when he was younger. But I had worked in this office for a year, and he never spoke more than two words, usually hello or how are you? But that was it. Oh, I also must point out that Amy said he was going through his mid-life crisis because he just bought a brand new Corvette. Anyway, I was standing there, trying not to make it any more awkward than it already was. I mean, his office was down the hall, but he knew Amy's father (an attorney) and the attorney I worked for as well. This was not the best situation for me. I told you I have this certain way of making men feel comfortable even when it's not. This was one of those times. I just smiled, and he started saying something else, but I didn't hear anything he was saying. I was just trying to figure out how to get out of the situation. He handed me his card. I took it and said, "Ok, thanks."

Finally, I saw Amy coming back down the hall from the bathroom. She got to us and said, "Ok, you ready?" I said, "Yeah." I looked at old Robert Dinero, and he said, "You ladies have a good lunch." When we got to the car, Amy looked at me and said, "What's going on? What did I miss?" So, I told her he asked me for my number, but before I could say anything, he gave me his card. I showed her the card, and his cell was on the back. Surprise.

Surprise. "What the fuck!" she said.

We got to the restaurant, a seafood spot that was kinda geared toward the older customers. You know what I'm talking about, retirees, because old folks luv them some seafood, and they can afford it. At least they can on this side of town. As we walked in, Amy was still fuming about what had happened.

"I can't believe that motherfucker!" she said.

Amy was very over-protective of me, so that's where this was coming from. I told her it was ok.

"No, it is not!" she said.

"Amy, for some reason, old white men seem to love me. It's not a big deal."

Before she could say anything else, the waiter came and said our table was ready. I followed the waiter, and Amy followed me. Ok, this place was filled with old white men. As I was walking, it was like all eyes were on me, and I could see Amy following everyone's eyes.

We got to our table, and Amy said, "WTF is going on here? Gaby, why is everyone looking at you?"

"It's no big deal," I said with a smile.

Before I could say anything else, here came an older WHITE gentleman.

"I don't mean to intrude, but I just want to tell you that you are a very beautiful woman," he said.

I just smiled and said, "Thank you. Very sweet of you to say." He smiled and walked back to his table.

Amy was sitting there with her mouth open. I guess because she'd never really paid attention before. All I said was, "See, no big deal." And this tends to happen from time to time. Now, back to my date.

I walked inside, and I looked toward the bar. I saw a man who waved at me, so I guessed that was my guy. Ok, ok, he looked like his pictures, with a little more salt in his hair than pepper. We sat at the bar, and it was a pretty full house, which wasn't unusual since it was a popular restaurant with really good food. He gave me a quick hug. I've always noticed white men like to hug and are quite touchy. He was all smiles and said, "Wow, you are gorgeous!" I thanked him and smiled. He asked me if I wanted a drink. Yes, definitely needed a drink. My drink was always the same, a sweet fruity drink. Fruity sweet not sour sweet. He got the bartender to make me a drink. Ok, conversation was good, he was making me laugh, so I was smiling a lot. I did notice that he was very handsy. Meaning, he had his hands on my back, then my shoulder, and then my leg. Handsy. Maybe it was my fault because I was laughing at all his jokes and was very engaged in his conversations. I know, nothing wrong with that, right? Only that I didn't know how I really felt about him. So, the longer I let it go on, the more he would think I was feeling him too. But shit, he was pretty funny, and I love to laugh. He was not a bad looking man, which is good. But there was something that didn't quite fit with him. I just hadn't quite put my finger on it. What I did know was that we had an audience from time to time, which again, was no surprise because of where we were. But this white man could have cared less. He was really happy to have my company. From time to time, he looked over at the looky lou's and said, "Isn't she just gorgeous?" And they couldn't help but smile.

I ordered my Hawaiian Ribeye... so, so good.

Oh, by the way, I just love food. Love, love to eat. I believe he quickly picked up on that. I guess he saw the look on my face while I was eating, like I was in heaven. He quickly jumped in and said, "I know this other restaurant that I would love to take you to. They have great French food."

"Oh wow, ok. I've never had French food, but I'll try it," I said.

I notice men always want to show me things I've never done or seen before. Interesting.

My stomach sometimes kept me dating men longer than I should have because of how well they fed me. A lot of times, food was the answer to a lot, and they knew it. Ok, we'd eaten, and it was about time to wrap it up. Oh, you're probably wondering what this man did for a living. He came from the Midwest and was retired. He sold some business he had, and I guess made a killing. Bought a house in AZ and never looked back.

We were walking out, and he pretty much had his hands all over me now. Not a good thing because I was feeling very uncomfortable. I could see he didn't catch or even care that I was. Then came the pressure for more. I got out of his chokehold and just smiled. I was trying to see how far the guy was willing to take it when I was not even giving him any green lights. Never mind. I definitely did not want to see how far he'd go because he was one of those men that won't get the 'not interested' hints.

We got to my car, and right away, he hugged me. Damn, you are not Brad Pitt or George Clooney, shit, or even Ben Affleck. He'd turned into an octopus. Dammit. I hate when this happens, but I would rather get this behavior sooner than later. And this guy couldn't control himself. Ok, so before I kicked him in the balls, I told him, "Ok, thank you for dinner. It was really nice meeting you."

"Yes, thank you for coming out, and I hope I can see you again," he said.

"I will call you," I said.

You know what I'm going to say, right. Seeing you again is a No for Me Dawg! Yup, Randy Jackson's back. Lol. Ok, I want to make this clear. The reason I would not be going out with ole Ted again was because I got the feeling he was looking for only one thing—a good time. Not because he was White. I was looking for a long-term relationship that could turn into marriage. I was not dating just to be dating. That is exactly what I said during our beginning conversations so there was no confusion. Most of the time, they would say they want the same thing, but then their actions tell me something else. The lesson here is do not ignore someone's actions. They are trying to tell you who they are. In this instance, it was not a White thing, it was a horndog thing.

I realized some men, not all, just don't have the discipline to engage in conversations, a little messaging, and a little patience in order to get what they want. I mean, even if you don't want the same thing, why not play along long enough to get what you want? I mean, don't get me wrong, thank the Lord I've never gotten myself into any bad situations, but I'm just saying communication, compliments, and some good food go a long way. I mean, you got me in the door, so to speak, then you ruin it with your stupid behavior. A lot of times I feel like saying, "You stupid, MutherFucker! You could've had some pussy!" Low Down Dirty Shame. I've always wanted to say that. Bahaha... Luv that movie. I mean, I'm not saying it would always work, but you know the times when it's a full moon, your hand is itching, the wind is blowing to the east, and your eye keeps twitching. Lol. The point is, you guys have missed a lot of opportunities if you would just pay attention and stop thinking you know how to get a woman. So, pay attention. I'm trying to help you guys out here. Damn.

Date

Alright, here we go again. Let's get back to Tinder dating. Ok, the swipe righters number was really growing, and it had only been a couple of days since I'd signed up. I know what you're thinking, there should be a lot of good matches since I have so many men interested. Right? And what I say to that is, not necessarily. I mean, I'm not saying these aren't good guys and/or catches. What I'm saying is just because there are a lot of eligible bachelors doesn't mean I am interested in them. Remember, the whole pictures and attraction thing. Well, that hasn't changed. I need to find you attractive in some kind of way, or what's the point? Ok, how about this one...

Roman, Black guy, worked for CBS, sounded interesting and pictures looked alright, good. I swiped right. Next thing you know, he sent me a message. We chit-chatted then exchanged numbers. Ok, so he was in town for work and staying in downtown Phoenix. He suggested we get together for drinks and possibly dinner in the next day or two. Ok, why not? We set up a date during the week, so I decided to play hooky from work. I mean, that's why the word hooky was invented, right? I agreed to meet him at the hotel bar where he was staying. I hate downtown parking remember, so I took an Uber instead of driving. I was pretty close by since, at that time, I was living in Central Phoenix. I got to the hotel and saw him sitting at the bar. I walked up, and he saw me. We greeted each other and sat down. Alright, I know what you're thinking. "Well... what did you think???" Unfortunately, he was a #3. I mean, it was definitely him. However, he had something weird going on with his hair. He definitely changed his hair because that shit was not in his pictures. It was like, you know, when men do the comb-over or the comb to the front when your hair is thinning. Well, it was kinda like that. It was combed to the front, but then it was like he had baby bangs. Let me just say, any kind of bangs on a dude is not a good look. Come on now, you are a Black man. How is it even possible to have bangs? Lol. You, Sir, look really crazy! How don't you see that in the mirror? Just wow. Oh, and his shirt was not buttoned all the way. You know when that last button is left unbuttoned. I don't even know why guys do that. Maybe they think it's sexy. Well, I assure you, it is so not. And in this case, his scrawny chest looked really cold in this desert air. So, there you have it.

Let's continue with my date. He finished his drink so we could go somewhere else because they only served drinks at the hotel, and I was hungry. I mean, if I am going to deal with you and your hair, oh and your little chest, I'm gonna need some food. Alright, here we go.

We were deciding whether to take an Uber or walk. And as we were waiting outside, trying to decide, one of those bicycle cabs came by. The one where there are seats attached to a guy that rides you around. Ok, in my mind, I was saying don't even think about it. I am not feeling this bullshit right now. I turned around to try and look in the other direction. I turned back around, and next thing I know, he was talking to the guy, and then he motioned over to me before I could object. Alright, this was some shit you do if you are liking the person you are with, which I was not. But fuck it, let's go get my meal.

We were riding through the city, and the guy was peddling his ass off, acting like it was a tour ride, talking about the city and the different places we passed. All I could think of was, Jesus, please take the bicycle wheel and get me out of this nightmare. We finally got to some Irish bar. Yup, and you guessed it, we were the only coloreds in the building, outside the building, under the building, or on the street.

"Is this ok, or do you want to go somewhere else?" he asked.

"This is fine," I said. Damn, I guess I'll have to help you fight when we get jumped.

He tried to get some small talk going while we were waiting for our drinks. First, he started by saying, "You are very pretty." I thanked him and said, "Please finish what you were saying."

He told me he worked for CBS (I was thinking to myself, I know. That's one of the main reasons I agreed to meet you). However, he told me he lucked up on getting his job, which was some sales job that he may or may not have for much longer. Welp, there goes that. Not that it mattered because I didn't even care if he was an anchor or the owner of CBS. This was not a match! He also told me he just got out of a relationship. But it sounded to me like he was still in it. He told me they had a very young child. Whew... so glad I dodged this bullet with bangs. I'm sorry, I just can't let it go. LMAO!!! He then started complaining about how she treated him. Sounded like she cheated on him because he started getting kind of worked up as he talked about her. Then he started making comments about sex and how the sex can only be good if you're in love with the person. I looked right at him and said, "Exactly!" But of course, he didn't get it because he just kept talking a lot more about nothing. Finally, the server came with the bill. I really needed for this to be over. Especially because I could see his little wheels turning, trying to come up with something to prolong the date.

He said, "You want to go somewhere else to have a drink?"

See, told you.

"No, I don't think so. I have work in the morning. I'll just catch an Uber back home."

"Do you want me to ride with you?" he asked.

Who are you and your bangs going to protect? Ok, ok, ok, I'm sorry. I can't take anymore, I just really needed to go.

"No, I'll be just fine," I said.

"Ok, I'll get the Uber for you," he offered.

Gee, thanks. We were waiting outside,

and I was looking around. You know how when you don't really want to make eye contact, so you don't have to keep talking. Yup, that was me. I saw the Uber and said loudly, "THERE IT IS!" I mean, there it is." Yikes... I sounded like I was happier to see the Uber than him. Oh well, that was what it was. I gave him a quick hug—you know the kind. I thanked him for dinner and pretty much threw myself in the car before he started talking again. Whew, and that was finally that.

A few days went by, and I didn't hear from him, so I guessed that meant he got it. So, I thought. The next night, which was a Saturday night, I got this text. His name popped up, so I knew it was him. I opened the text, and it was a video of him singing. I guess he was serenading me. It was an R Kelly song, but I don't know the name of the song. I do remember he had a white hat and black gloves on. Something about I'm on bended knee. That man had lost his damn mind. SMDH. But that was it. I never heard from him again. This was just not a match.

Nothing too crazy. I mean, it was him in his pictures, but him live and in person didn't translate well from his pictures to real life. I really didn't know him well enough to even say if he was a good guy or not. But from his conversations, let's just say it was a good thing it wasn't a match because I probably would have ended up hurting his little feelings by cutting his bangs off in his sleep. Ok. Ok. Ok, now I'm done.

Ok, just so you know, these are not consecutive dates I was going on. I am not a serial dater. I went on these dates over long periods of time. Like over the course of years. I don't want you thinking I'm just a dating machine because I definitely am not. And once I met someone I was interested in, I only date that one guy. Just wanted to set the record straight before you slander my name in these streets.

Date

Michael is a former NFL player I met on Tinder. From his pictures, it was obvious he was affiliated with football. One of his pictures was him on a football field and him waving to the crowd with a big crowd and media in the background. Another picture was him and Evander Holyfield. I couldn't really tell where he was, if it was a football field or boxing arena. It was too close of a shot. Anyway, you get the picture. I swiped right. He had already swiped right, so I knew he was interested.

I messaged him my usual, "Hey there, how's it going?" And he responded, so we started brief messaging. I say brief because he didn't really have much conversation. More like, so what do you like to do? And where do you like to go? So, when I get that, I wanted to meet up and get to it instead of more annoying bullshit. I mean, you never know, in person it might turn out to be better. I have found that sometimes, men don't communicate very well through text, and some don't like to, so their answers are very short. Let's see which one ole Michael is.

We'd decided to meet for lunch at the same restaurant I met up with White Ted, remember. Yup, my idea. I was in my business casual attire. I got there and it was pretty busy as usual. He was already there. I was taken to his table, and we greeted each other. He was also coming from work, and I saw he was also in business casual attire. He had on plaid pants, kind of loud, but it worked. As we started our conversation, someone came over and said, "Michael, hey, how are you?" Michael got up and shook his hand. The man saw me and said, "I will give you a call so we can catch up," and he left.

By then, I was thinking, ok, ok, he seems

to be known around here because there was another man who came over to say hi as well. It kind of made me want to get to know what he was all about. We ordered drinks—just tea, people, it was only lunchtime. We started talking about the usual, where you're from, your interests, and what you do for a living. You know, the usual. I asked him where he had traveled to because one of his pictures looked like he was in Russia. Then our food came. I started to eat.

"You seem kind of quiet," he said.

I looked at him, and I was thinking, well, that's because right now I'm eating. But instead, I said, "Well, we've been talking so far, so not sure what you mean by that?"

"Oh, right," he said.

Ok, his personality was not very outgoing, so maybe he was used to women being more forward with him. I guess since he was a former athlete. I wanted to say, well, sir, I am definitely not the throw-myself-at-you kind of girl/groupie type. I think he quickly found that out. I mean, shit, we were having lunch and getting to know each other conversations. And for me, I was really just seeing if there would even be a second date kind of conversations. Just being honest here. Remember, if there is no kind of

246

chemistry or vibe, I don't really care that you're a former anything, it's going to be a no for me.

Ok, I know you're wondering about his looks, right? Well, he was alright. I was honestly hoping he would look better in person, but he looked exactly like his pictures. So, there were no surprises there. Was I instantly attracted to him? No...I was not. But he had this kind of insecure thing about him that made me want to talk to him and know more about him. I don't know if that even makes sense, but that's what I was feeling. We finished our lunch and walked out, and we got to my car.

"I would like to see you again," he said with a quick hug.

"Ok, call me, and we'll get together again," I said, and I wasn't lying.

Like I said, I wouldn't mind knowing more about him. He didn't have the usual personality of an athlete. At least not the few I'd met. They are definitely not shy at all. And he kind of was, so I appreciated that.

As I was driving back to work, I got a text. Michael. He said, 'it was nice meeting you. You are very pretty.' See shy. He didn't say any of that in person. I didn't even know if he liked me.

A couple of weeks later, we were finally free to go on a second date. It was a Friday night, so we decided to go to dinner. I told him the area I lived, so he picked a restaurant somewhere in the middle. You know how I feel about the meeting in the middle thing. It tells me that you don't like going out of your way, and that tells me you're not really trying all that hard at accommodating a woman. And from what I'd experienced in the past, that was never a good sign. But, ok, whatever.

I got to the restaurant, and it was crowded. We chose to sit at the bar instead of waiting for a table, which was totally fine with me. We started talking, and I asked him about his football days. "I'd like to hear stories about your sports life." We got to talking, and he told me some pretty interesting stuff about some players and also about the dating pool for athletes. I always wondered why I saw a lot of athletes and celebrities get with the same women. Like she was being passed around. Ewww.

He told me it was hard to trust women when you reached a certain level, so they would rather be with someone that was known to be trusted and loyal instead of getting with an outsider with questionable loyalty or unknown trust/loyalty, which made sense, I guess, maybe to a male. But to me, not all that much.

"So, you would rather have someone that everyone else has had instead of someone no one has been with?" I asked. That made no sense to me. But whatever. I didn't really give a shit either way. Let us move on.

Ok, I was still on the fence as to whether I wanted to see him again because I was still getting the same dry personality from him. We finished up and headed out to our cars. We got to my car, and we were chit-chatting about what was next. I told him to call me, and we'd get together again. I mean, not really sure what was next because he didn't really talk about how he felt or what he was wanting with me. We pretty much had a meal and chit-chatted while we were eating, then it was over. Nothing more, nothing less. A little strange. I gave him a hug, but this time he held on a little longer than the last time I had seen him. And yup, he went in for the kill. I turned my head, so he landed on my cheek. But I gave him another hug because I saw the look of a little boy who didn't get a toy at the toy store on his face, and it made me feel bad.

"Call me so we can plan to get together

again when you are free, ok," I said.

He said, "ok," and then I got in my car and drove off.

Well, damn. I didn't think he was gonna try and kiss me. You know, since I wasn't giving him the please kiss me vibe. You know, there is such a vibe. But I always think when in doubt, don't do it! I guess I was wrong. Ok. Ok. Ok. I know what you're thinking... Bitch, you are not interested in him! Stop playing games.

First of all, I don't play games. Second, I told you I was kind of interested, that's why I agreed to see him again. But I will be honest. I think what kept my interest was the fact that he was a former athlete, and that brought a certain excitement. Right. Well, whatever. Fuck you guys. Lol. Unfortunately, with this guy, I wasn't getting any kind of personality, it was just blah. When it gets like pulling teeth, it's time to be out. And honestly, it was almost that time. And he said I was quiet. Ok, one more time, and that's it. If nothing changes, then I am totally done.

We chit-chatted more on the phone via text because I felt like if we talked on the phone, we would never make it to a third date. I know, sad. But it was what it was. The next weekend we were both free, and we couldn't decide where to go. He suggested the movies, but there wasn't really anything playing. I thought a movie was probably not a good idea because there was no talking, and we wouldn't be able to get to know each other. Oh, and I have to point out, he was a little weird about me knowing where he lived. Like when I asked him what side of town he lived in. He said the north side. Then I said, "OK, exactly where like what streets because that's vague." Instead of telling me, he asked where I lived. He acted like he was paranoid for anyone to know that. As if I would figure out where his exact house was and go there or stalk him. I know, crazy, right? At first, I thought maybe it was because I was a total stranger, but we'd been out a couple of times, and we'd talked. You should clearly see I am not a crazy stalker type. Then I thought maybe he'd had bad experiences with women because he was a former football player. I didn't really know, but you, sir, are coming off like a scary weirdo. Anyway, I told him where I lived, and he suggested the casino since there was one close to me on my side of town. I said, "Ok, yeah, that sounds good. I wouldn't mind playing a little blackjack."

I got to the casino about 8:30 p.m. or so,

and I was looking pretty good, I might add. I had long shorts on that were fitted in the right places with heels. I was walking through the casino, and I spotted ole Michael at the bar. Oh, if I didn't mention before, Michael was about 7 years my senior. He was sitting at a bar. He saw me walking up, and he got up to give me a hug. We started chit-chatting, a lot about nothing really. I got the feeling he was trying to figure out how to keep my attention because, honestly, we were running out of things to say, and that is never a good sign. Nothing really flows naturally without coming to an awkward silence.

This time he told me how good I looked. Shocker. I thought maybe he was thinking it was the last chance for anything to happen, which he was right. We ordered a couple of drinks.

"So, what do you want to play?" I asked.

"I like the slots," he said and then asked me. I like blackjack. I'm not great at it, but I can hold my own. Ok. Ok. Ok. Let me ask you this, when a man invites you on a date to the casino, do you expect him to give you money to play with? Is that not implied, or is this just me? I surely expected to get some dollars to get started. Ok, so this is what happened with Michael. Yes, the Michael who invited me to the casino on a 3rd date. That Michael. We walked over to the blackjack tables so I could pick a lucky table. I was looking, got some looks from players and dealers. Then I finally picked one. I sat down, and old Michael was behind me. Ok, the hand is dead, and the dealer was looking at me like 'are you going to get in on this or not?' I smiled at him, and I paused for a minute, but really, I was waiting for Michael to hand over some money. You know, because I am here with him, on a date. But nope, not a peep from him. He didn't even reach for his wallet. I went into my purse and put a one-hundred-dollar bill on the table. I was thinking, this sorry muthafucker, I knew he wasn't shit! But you know what, I am going to enjoy myself and try to win me some money.

After a few hands, he said, "Ok, I'll be at the slots." I nodded my head. Fuckin' weirdo, why did you even invite me if you were going to be doing your own thing? I had this disgusted look on my face. Then I looked at the dealer, and the dealer was looking at me, and he gave me this look like, 'you're right, he definitely ain't shit!' Lol. Then I was ready to have a good time. And so, I did.

The dealer kept giving me the eye. I mean, he was ugly, but who cared, we were having a good time. I won some hands, but then I lost them. You know how it goes. After an hour or so, Michael's ass showed back up. He came up to me and said, "I think I'm going to head out." I turned to look at him, and I said, "Ok, take care." And that was the end of Michael.

He texted me a few times, but I didn't answer because I knew if I did, I would have said something nasty. You know what, people? I don't even care what you think. I do not feel bad for believing that a man who takes you out to a casino should at least offer you money to play with, especially if he is the one who invited you there.

Now because of that experience, the next times I was invited to the casino, I made it perfectly clear that I was not going to be using my own money. And believe it or not, they all agreed with me, that I shouldn't.

Date

I responded to a message. Ron. I felt like I had run across him before, so I decided to take a good look. Nice looking dude, had about 5 pictures in different settings. I responded to his message. Another Phoenix local, so that was good. We quickly exchanged numbers and started chit-chatting. He had just relocated to Phoenix from Idaho. He had only been in Arizona a couple of months and moved here by himself. I felt some sympathy for him because he was here by himself. He seemed to be a pretty outgoing guy, which was cool. He wanted to meet up pretty quickly, and I was all for it.

You know how I feel about wasting time. As we were deciding where to meet, we continued talking about our backgrounds. He told me he had a child who lived here with the mother. She was 3. Damn, that was really young. Normally, my rule of thumb is no kids under 10. My experience is small children bring a lot of issues/drama. I know I am not perfect, but I really try to avoid getting involved with anyone with small children. I don't have any baby daddy issues and never have. This is my personal preference. Ok, so let's just see what happens.

I was off work that day, so we decided to meet up for lunch, and then we would go from there. I arrived at Raw, a sushi spot. I don't eat sushi, but they have some good cooked rolls. As I was pulling in, I saw a bright yellow Camaro drive up behind me, and I saw a Black dude inside. What I was thinking at that very minute was, damn, that's probably him. What also popped in my mind was the Transformers Bumble Bee, and that is not a compliment. Every time I saw a bright yellow car, I just thought, who needs a car that bright? Someone who definitely wants to be seen. But then I thought to myself, it's just a Camaro, not a Ferrari. Why do you need all that attention? Ok, maybe it's not him. I got out and started walking, but then I saw him park and get out of the Bumble Bee, I mean the yellow Camaro. Shit. All I could think about right now was, if we get together, I am going to have to ride with him in this attention seeker? Oh well, it is what it is.

I got to the door, and here he comes. "Hey, how's it going?" I wanted to ask him, why do you have a bright, loud ass yellow car? Why? Ok, I'm not going to be mean. We got seated, and we ordered drinks. He started with, "Man, you are just as beautiful as your pictures. Really you're even more beautiful in person." I thanked him. And I guess that was the part where I was supposed to tell him about himself. You know I don't like to lie, but I don't like to be mean either.

"I really like that you had different pictures and not just one selfie," I told him.

He smiled and started talking about where he took each one. Most guys do like talking about themselves. Really funny how most guys I meet always talk about themselves but don't notice that I don't talk about myself unless it's when I'm asked a question. I just let them talk. Then we kind of got into the "pictures" conversation. I told him, "You know, people fall into 3 categories when it comes to pictures.

"Oh, really, what are those?" he asked.

"1) You look just/exactly like your picture, 2) You look better than your picture; or, 3) You look worse than your picture. That's it."

"Oh wow," he said. I could see him thinking about it. He then smiled and said, "You are right, that totally makes sense."

Shit, I knew what he was going to ask me. "So, what number am I?"

I knew it. Never fails. This is me, trying not to be mean or crush someone's ego.

"You look just like your pictures," I said with a kind of smile.

"Oh, good, I'm glad," he said with a smile.

Alright, let's get this out of the way. He was about 5'10" in pretty good shape. Black. But I was not really feeling him. Truthfully, I didn't feel anything. Sorry, people. He seemed like a nice guy. Kind of on the eager beaver side. Like he was fishing for conversation when I got quiet. You know, so it wouldn't end. I am serious when I say he was a nice guy. But no physical attraction here. The only question for me was if I wanted to be his friend or nothing. When I say friend, I mean someone to hang out with because remember he told me he was out here in the desert alone. I was not really sure. But this guy, knew exactly what he wanted with me because he kept telling me he was so glad I responded to his message and that we'd met. Alright, alright, sometimes I'm a sucker. I agreed to go to the movies with him since I was off and didn't have any plans. We found a movie and then we rode in the same car. SMH. Fine, fuck it, I'm a Bumble Bee too!

We arrived at the theatre and got popcorn and drinks. Everything was fine. It was going well, no issues or surprises. We were watching previews, and one was a scary movie. He got really panicky. This grown ass man was afraid of scary movies. I don't mean he just didn't watch them. I mean, he was SCARED of them! I mean, he was all jumpy, and when I looked at him, he had this really scared look on his face like a terrified little boy. I was like, damn nigga, get a hold of yourself, because if you embarrass me, I am walking out. There, it was over. I guess he realized how crazy he was looking, so he apologized. BTW, I love scary movies, and that is not how you are supposed to act when you watch one, even if it is a good, scary one.

The movie started, and we were into it. As time went on, he got real quiet. When I looked over to him, he was asleep. Yes, asleep on our first date. SMDH. He jumped a couple of times. I looked at him and shook my head. After the movie, as we were walking out, we looked at each other, and burst into laughter at his crazy ass. He mentioned a club he wanted to go to that night. He was doing all the talking because I didn't know if I even wanted to see ole Sleepy Hollow again.

On the drive back to my car, he kept talking to get me to agree to go out with him that night. We finally got to my car, and before I could say anything, he said, "Ok, I'll pick you up at 8:30, ok?"

I looked at him and saw this sad, please, please, say yes, look on his face. So, I just said, "Alright." And just like that, he took off in his Transformers Bumble Bee Camaro.

I was getting ready to go out, and I was actually excited to get out and have a good time. Look, I like to go out once in a while, and believe it or not, a lot of men I run across do not like going out at all. They'll say, "Oh, I used to hit the clubs back in the day, but I don't do that anymore." FYI, anyone who says, "I used to hit the clubs back in the day," is too old for me anyway. Just saying. I don't hit the clubs on the regular, but I do like to get dressed up for a night on the town. Or I've also heard, "I don't do clubs, but I'll do a lounge or a bar." Again, you're too old for me, Sir. Why not take me out once in a while if that's what I like? That's why I don't want you.

So anyway, I was getting ready. I decided to wear jeans, a nice low cut, tight top, heels, and a leather jacket because it was cold that night. Nothing too fancy but definitely club attire. Besides, I knew the spot we were going to. It was an old spot with an older crowd, from what I remembered. Hadn't been there in years, but I did remember that they played good music. He texted me that he had arrived. I went outside, and he got out to open my door. This is the sight I saw in front of me. He was wearing jeans, which was cool. I couldn't really see what kind of shirt he had on, if it was a dress shirt or what, because all I could see was this jacket he had on with fringe on the sleeves. You remember the movie Dumb and Dumber when Lloyd was wearing that country western-looking jacket? Well, that pattern but with fringe on the sleeves. All I could think of was, why did I agree to this shit? I am a modern kind of girl, and nothing about me says country or western. Or that I like any of that. Well, I guess it could have been worse, he could've been wearing a cowboy hat. SMDH. Anyway, here I fuckin' go.

We got there, and yes, it was the spot I was thinking about. It was about 10:00 p.m. there weren't very many people. It looked like a spot that people had forgotten about or go to when their original plans had fallen through. That kind of spot. We walked in, and I got a few looks. You know, like, 'hmmm... this don't match' kind of looks. Or 'damn, what is she doing in here?' And I was in the whatever, I am just here to have some drinks and listen to good music mood. Not sure what was on his mind. I'm lying. I knew what was on his mind because he was looking at me like a little boy who had just found his lost dog. I kept looking away, and if he didn't stop looking at me with that smile, I was going to leave. He must have sensed my "boy, you better get it together vibe" because he stopped staring at me and ordered us drinks.

We were at a table where we could see everything in the whole club. I could see people coming in and out. The music was getting good, and after a glass, I was feeling pretty good. I was looking around, and I saw a few men that I caught checking me out. They looked at me, then they looked at Willie Nelson across from me. I really wondered what they were thinking. I turned back to Ron, and he was already looking at me. Damn, it was going to be a long night.

I got up to go to the bathroom, and on my way back to my table, a guy walked up to me. He grabbed my hand and said, "Hey, how you doing? I saw you when I came in." I said, "Then you must have noticed I was not alone." He just looked at me and said, "Oh, you mean Roy Rogers at your table?" Ok, just so you know, even if I didn't have any intentions of being with Ron in any capacity, I would never disrespect him since I had come with him. So, that being said, I told the guy I wasn't interested, and I headed back to my table. I'm the only one who can talk shit about him because you don't know him like that. But I had to admit, "Roy Rogers" was pretty funny. Lol.

After a few more songs, I told Ron I was ready to go. We headed back to my place. On the ride home, he was pretty quiet. I knew that silence all too well. It was the Dead Man Walking silence. It was the silence when the guy realizes there was not going to be another date or nothing at all was happening in the future tense. I hated these drives. But not bad enough to change my mind about seeing you again.

I said goodnight and goodbye. And so that was the end of Ron and his jacket.

CHAPTER TWELVE: DAMN

All the stories in this book are TRUE STORIES. This crazy shit actually happened to me. Some were "Shake your damn head" damn, this shit really happened stories, and some were WOWSER, that's some funny shit stories. But nevertheless, they are all true, people! What I am trying to tell you is that you cannot make this shit up, and neither can I.

I know some of you can totally relate to some of the stories about random meetings. I am pretty sure you have been approached in a similar fashion. I am not claiming to be the most beautiful woman in the world but attractive is attractive. And when people take notice of you on a regular basis, that is your proof. Now, you will run across men who don't want to admit to your "fineness" (new word I just made up), but those are the ones who most likely want you and can't have you. Trust me, I know all about that. And if they don't want to admit it to you, just tell them to look around whenever you are out and about. You will notice random people looking at you wherever you go. They don't even have to approach you. It's a kind of an aura/vibe you give off that makes people take notice. You get looks and stares, and they are non-threatening. It's kind of a curiosity of them wanting to know who you are.

When I was younger, my wise old Aunt Tillie once told me, when I was fed up with being whistled at or disturbed. She said, "Honey, men look at you and see a beautiful woman. You don't know what kind of life they have at home, but when they see you, you make their day by maybe giving them a fantasy or just a smile just for that moment. So, give them that. What does it hurt?" I really thought about it, and she was right, what did it hurt? After that, I looked at it just like that, and most of the time, I even smile back.

Start paying attention to your surroundings, and you will notice what I mean. These are facts. I know I am not alone in this. I believe the level of attractiveness really depends on the amount of attention you get. Whenever you are at the grocery store, the gas station, the airport, etc. Even your friends should be able to confirm this.

And if your friends are also attractive, then you will get double the attention. I am just trying to put all of this into context for you so you understand where I'm coming from.

As far as the dating and relationships, I went into all of them with an open mind and an open heart. When I started my journey, I was coming out of my divorce. There is never an easy way to deal with divorce. Even more terrifying was the idea of getting out there and dating again. However, during the time I was re-entering the dating pool, the whole internet dating was beginning to really catch fire. I was pretty excited and hopeful that I would find my prince charming. And in the "beginning," I was having a blast meeting men from different places that I would have never run across on my own.

Unfortunately, slowly but surely, the whole dating dance started to lose its steam. I don't know about you, but I definitely felt like I was on a rollercoaster ride. The ups and downs and a lot of shit in between. I mean, all the non-attraction, the over exaggerations, and then the deceit. Damn, that deceit shit was really crazy. But along the way, I have learned not to take life so seriously, especially when dating. Well, this is actually a must to avoid going insane.

I also learned that laughter is definitely the best medicine. I am doing a lot of just that these days. I am enjoying each person I meet and the different experiences that come along the way. I rarely play the blame game, except when a muthafucker totally changes the rules of the game without any warning. Although it got very discouraging at times, it was never enough for me to give up on finding everlasting true love. I know, I just made myself throw up too. Lol!

I am still surviving out here in the dating world. I am still standing strong and still looking for my prince charming. And so, the journey continues. . .

ABOUT THE AUTHOR

Gabriela Zion is a Southern California native, born in Duarte and raised in San Bernardino. She migrated to Arizona with her husband and there she raised three children. The Loves of her life. In her free time, she plays tennis and is a lover of sports. A true romantic, you can find her reading random romance novels or binge watching anything on the Hallmark channel.

After her divorce she took time to heal and rediscover herself and then reentered the dating world to find the elusive "Mr. Right." Gabriela has spent decades in the law profession fostering her long held aspiration of sharing her writing with an audience eager for an honest voice. She began writing as a way of coming to grips with the fact that dating is an anomaly. Her material, always candid and truthful, speaks from her experiences while highlighting the oftentimes strange points of view of the men she's encountered. Gabriela has dated men from all walks of life and presents a fresh perspective on an age-old question... "What do women really want?"

Easy on the eyes and even easier on the

ears, Gabriela is a new author writing for today's modern reader. She still believes LOVE is always the answer and refuses to believe otherwise.

Discover more about Gabriela and her book on:

Website   gabrielazion.com

and her social media:

Instagram   @gabriela_zion

Twitter   @gabriela_zion

 Facebook author.gabrielazion

272

Made in the USA
Columbia, SC
15 February 2024

31539991R00154